What people are saying about …

JUMP

"From one of the most important voices of the next evangelicalism comes this practical, accessible, and important guide to the Christian spiritual life. Drawing upon humorous illustrations and real-life examples from his years of ministry experience, Efrem provides a challenge and a hope for many of us who have been afraid to jump. In addition, Efrem's willingness to share personal stories yields a sensitive and authentic insight into the dynamics of race and cross-cultural ministry in the American church. *Jump* confirms Efrem Smith's role as one of the most important evangelical voices for the twenty-first century."

Soong-Chan Rah, Milton B. Engebretson
associate professor of church growth
and evangelism, North Park Theological
Seminary, and author of *The Next
Evangelicalism* and *Many Colors*

"Pastor Efrem is a gifted communicator, and that God-given talent has come through very well in print. After reading this piece, the one word that rings strongest in my spirit is *inspiring!* Pastor Efrem has captured a powerful image through his illustrations and storytelling—a missing key that will help unlock and free many people who are bound up in life by their fears and the lies the Enemy has fed them. I believe Efrem's transparency about his spiritual journey with its tests and triumphs will be inspiring and liberating to readers from many walks of life."

"Efrem Smith takes the reader on a journey from personal transformation to community transformation in this new book. He helps us see possibilities beyond barriers and stumbling blocks. Then he guides us into practical ways we can experience new life in Christ personally and in the richness of a multicultural experience of community that God intends for His people. Anyone who reads this book will gain a new perspective on the breadth and depth of God's grace applied to our daily experiences."

"Pastor Efrem Smith is one of God's chosen leaders for a new generation of Christ followers. As I read *Jump*, he had me literally on the edge of my seat with both excitement and newfound understanding of God and the beloved community. I highly recommend this book—it can transform our lives, and the life of the church."

JUMP

JUMP

INTO A

LIFE OF

FURTHER AND

HIGHER

EFREM SMITH

David C Cook®

transforming lives together

JUMP
Published by David C. Cook
4050 Lee Vance View
Colorado Springs, CO 80918 U.S.A.

David C. Cook Distribution Canada
55 Woodslee Avenue, Paris, Ontario, Canada N3L 3E5

David C. Cook U.K., Kingsway Communications
Eastbourne, East Sussex BN23 6NT, England

David C. Cook and the graphic circle C logo
are registered trademarks of Cook Communications Ministries.

Unless otherwise noted, Scripture quotations are taken from the *New American
Standard Bible*, © Copyright. 1960, 1995 by The Lockman Foundation.
Used by permission. Scripture quotations marked NIV are taken from the *New
International Version*. *NIV*. Copyright © 1973, 1978, 1984 by International
Bible Society. Used by permission of Zondervan. All rights reserved.

LCCN 2010930461
ISBN 978-1-4347-6457-7
eISBN 978-1-4347-0253-1

© 2010 Efrem Smith
Published in association with the Eames Literary Services.llc, Nashville, TN.

The Team: John Blase, Amy Kiechlin, Jack Campbell, Karen Athen
Cover Design: JuiceBox Design, Jay Smith

Printed in the United States of America
First Edition 2010

1 2 3 4 5 6 7 8 9 10

070110

I dedicate this book to the Sanctuary Covenant Church and Community Development Corporation. It was such a joy to serve as senior pastor and CDC president of this evangelical, multiethnic, missional, and urban ministry.

Contents

ACKNOWLEDGMENTS

There are so many people I would like to acknowledge who were helpful in this book's coming together.

I'm thankful to Don Pape at David C. Cook for believing in my ability to continue my writing and take it to another level. The editing and suggestions of John Blase are also something I'm very thankful for.

I consider many people mentors in the shaping of my theology and practical ministry outlooks: Brenda Salter-McNeil, Dave Olson, Curtiss DeYoung, Gerald Joiner, Gary Walter, Don Davenport, Pete Scazerro, Daryl Griffin, Henry Greenidge, Tom Paige, Keith Johnson, Sherwood Carthen, John Perkins, and Greg Boyd, to name a few. Reading their works and listening to them have had a tremendous impact on me.

I want to acknowledge the staff of the Sanctuary Covenant Church with whom I've had the opportunity to share so much of my ministry passion and life. I have much love for all of you. I'm grateful to the staff and pastors of the Pacific Southwest Conference who have embraced me and welcomed me as their new servant-leader.

Finally, I want to thank the three beautiful and wonderful ladies in my life—my wife, Donecia, and my daughters, Jaeda and Mireya. My love for you is beyond what I could ever effectively communicate.

INTRODUCTION

As I prepared to write a book on faith jumping, I never thought I would be making one of my own before the book was even released. After serving for seven and a half years as the senior pastor of the Sanctuary Covenant Church in Minneapolis, Minnesota, I was presented the opportunity to serve as the next superintendent of the Pacific Southwest Conference of the Evangelical Covenant Church. In this role I will oversee the churches and other ministry initiatives of the Evangelical Covenant Church in California, Arizona, Hawaii, Nevada, and Utah. I'm so humbled and honored to have been elected to serve in this position. I will start, full steam ahead, at the same time that this book is released.

This was not an easy decision for me to make. I have enjoyed so much serving as the senior pastor of the Sanctuary Covenant Church. I'm also the founding pastor of this church, which was planted to be intentionally evangelical, multiethnic, and urban. Add to that, Minneapolis is also the place where I was born and raised.

As I prayed about going through the process to be considered for the superintendent role, I thought about the opportunity to see on a broader scale the ministry fruit I have experienced at Sanctuary. I continue to have a passion to see the Kingdom of God advanced in an ever-increasing multiethnic and multicultural world. I also yearn to see a stronger connection between evangelism, discipleship, compassion, mercy, and justice. Making this connection is about embracing the whole mission of God. The region of the Evangelical Covenant Church presents the opportunity to see this connection thrive in mighty ways. The West Coast is a powerful expression of diversity and also a platform for further Kingdom advancement and transformation. My passion and this opportunity of servant-leadership is what led me to the jump into a new calling and season of ministry.

Taking the jump into a new Kingdom opportunity is not always easy. I cannot even begin to express how tough it was to share the news of my departure to a congregation and community that I love so much. If a pastor can easily leave a church he has served, he has neither a love for the people nor a true understanding of what it means to be a pastor. It's difficult making various jumps in life, even those that have been prayed through. Yet God is in the business at times of giving us the invitation to jump into opportunities that call for a trusting of Him in new ways. I'm excited, as well as nervous and overwhelmed, to take on this new role. These feelings are all good if they lead to trusting God in a deeper way. God doesn't want us to just jump for jumping's sake. We shouldn't live a life that says, "Look at what a great and holy jumper I am!"

Our jumps should be based on God's speaking to us; they should be jumps of obedience. Also these jumps ought to increase our dependence on and trust of God. All of this leads to the deepening of our intimacy with God, a clearer identity in Christ, and a stronger sense of the indwelling of the Holy Spirit. The big issue to embrace here is that we don't jump alone. We jump with God and empowered by God. God is the "spring" in the jump, and God should also be in control of our landing. We can't always clearly see the landing point, but God sees it all. There are parts of the landing out west that I can see. I experience times of excitement as I look in anticipation at these landing points. I see a gifted and diverse staff that I get to work with. I see a Hispanic theological school. I see a cool Kingdom initiative called Journey to Mosaic that equips people to become Kingdom laborers in an age of increasing diversity. I see camps and conference centers. I see eager church planters. Okay, let me just put it out there, I see ministry trips to Hawaii! But for a Minnesotan like me, Phoenix and San Diego are awesome trips.

There are also times when we will sense strongly that scary feeling of being still in the air. That's how I'm feeling as I write this. I'm not yet in California, I haven't yet bought a new home, and I don't know where my daughters will be going to school. Neither I nor Sanctuary knows who the next senior pastor will be. All of this up-in-the-air time drives me to my loving Father. Jumping brings me closer to my Daddy in heaven. Oh, the scary joy of jumping!

Where is God calling you to take jumps of faith in your life? I hope this book ministers to you as you ponder the jumps God is calling you into. Maybe you find it hard to give yourself over to letting God get you off the ground. I can relate. As I thought about the jump to serve as a superintendent within a denomination, there were many things going through my head that could have kept me grounded. One, I was concerned about what the folks at Sanctuary would think of me. Would they be mad at me? Would people feel abandoned by me? I wondered what other pastors would think of me. Would they think I was crazy for taking this jump?

It's important for us to remember that we have good company. What did people think of Peter when he took the jump to leave his business and follow Jesus? What did people think of Jeremiah when he took the jump to be God's prophetic voice to a disobedient nation? What did people think of Esther when she decided not to be a passive queen simply serving the will of the king? Her jump saved the lives of an entire people. Our jumps may not turn out to be that big, but God is in all of them just the same.

I'm excited to serve the Evangelical Covenant Church this way. This denomination has taken a leap of its own in being willing to present a different picture of evangelicalism. It's important to see a denomination that believes in the authority of Scripture, the necessity of new birth, and the importance of discipleship and that embraces the biblical mandate of justice. When I think of the opportunity to serve those values, it's hard to keep my feet on the ground! Yes, I'm jumping....

Chapter 1

THE IMPALA

My pastor friend Darrell once told me a story that has given me a new vision for living the Christian life. Not long ago Darrell took his son to the zoo and became intrigued with an animal known as the African impala. It just so happened that a female staffer from the zoo was standing near the enclosure giving background information on the impala, so he stopped to listen. I must be honest and say that at that point in my life the only thing I knew about an impala was that Chevrolet made them. As I said, Darrell is my friend. He could tell my thoughts of Chevy automobiles were distracting me from really listening to his story. But he's also a pastor, so he put his hand on my shoulder to regain my attention.

The zookeeper told Darrell and his son some interesting facts about the impala. She said this animal has the ability to jump thirteen feet high in the air from a standing position. This allows the impala to escape predators that try to sneak up on it from behind. The impala has the ability to jump not only up but also out—thirty feet out. An impala's back is like a shock absorber, which is crucial since the animal's leaps are like explosions. Impalas can reach maximum running speeds of close to sixty miles per hour. Again, a natural survival skill. But it was what the woman said next that really caught Darrell's attention. "Notice that even though the impala has the ability to jump thirteen feet high and thirty feet out, the African impalas are contained here at the zoo by a three-foot wall!"

This grabbed my attention too. "Stop right there! How is it that an animal with the ability to jump thirteen feet high and thirty feet out can be contained by a three-foot wall?" I asked.

Darrell went on to explain that when the impalas are young, they are taught they can't jump over the three-foot wall. Zoo personnel do this by emphasizing a weakness of the adults. An adult impala is hesitant to use its ability to jump if it is unable to see where it's going to land. The inability to see the end of the jump somehow hinders the impala from something it is naturally able to do. I'm a pastor too, like Darrell, so let me put it this way: The inability to live by faith keeps the impala from doing what God created it to do, what it was born to do. It grows up to become an adult with the ability to jump into freedom, to live out its purpose, but it won't because it doesn't believe it can. Darrell finished his story there and said, "Anytime you want to use that in a sermon, feel free." I've been connecting that story to every sermon ever since.

The Christian life in so many ways is about a series of jumps that can take us higher and further into a life of intimacy with and identity in Christ. The Christian life is about the love relationship that God desires to have with us, so that we become His beloved, advancing the Kingdom of God on earth. And on many days this involves taking leaps of faith into the unknown.

From my pastoral point of view, I look around today and see believers all across the land behind three-foot walls. Like African impalas, they've been taught one thing or another, many times things completely unscriptural, that keeps them from jumping into the life God wants for them.

For example, maybe they're taught early on that Christianity is a bunch of rules, and if you don't follow the rules, God doesn't love you. I know for a fact that this has kept more than one Christian from ever knowing the freedom of jumping into an intimate relationship with God. Or maybe some people were warned not to learn about spiritual gifts. As a result, they have never taken the leap into knowing their spiritual gifts and God-given mission to advance the Kingdom of heaven on earth.

All that explosive God-potential just sitting behind a three-foot wall.

I think about the life of Peter in the gospel of John as a picture of this. In the first chapter, Andrew, Peter's brother, brings him to meet Jesus:

One of the two who heard John speak, and followed Him, was Andrew, Simon Peter's brother. He found

first his own brother Simon and said to him, "We have
found the Messiah" (which translated means Christ).
He brought him to Jesus. Jesus looked at him and said,
"You are Simon the son of John; you shall be called
Cephas" (which is translated Peter).

John 1:40–42

Peter had to make a decision to take the jump of following
Jesus without fully knowing where this jump would end. Yet these
jumps into the unknown are the key to freedom in Christ and our
ability to advance the Kingdom of God on earth. Peter had to
deal with some three-foot walls in making the initial decision to
follow Jesus. Maybe his three-foot wall was leaving his fishing
business behind. Or maybe it was dealing with what his friends
and other family members would think of him for following one
who proclaimed to be the Son of God. Whatever the specifics,
it's clear Peter had to deal with a three-foot wall of some kind in
making his initial jump. When we make the decision to follow
Christ, we have to deal with a three-foot wall of some kind too.

But as many as received Him, to them He gave the right
to become children of God, even to those who believe in
His name, who were born, not of blood nor of the will
of the flesh nor of the will of man, but of God.

John 1:12–13

We may not be able to see what's on the other side of the wall, but we know one thing: God is there. We are, by faith, jumping into God's love! We can't see God, but we hear His voice on the other side calling us into love, forgiveness, and freedom.

Though freedom waits for us on the other side, the walls around us can be overwhelming. Three-foot walls often feel more like skyscrapers. This is one reason why we must be loving and patient with people who have not yet come to know Jesus as Lord and Savior. We don't know what they've been through. We don't know the multiple walls they may be facing as they consider this faith jump. Evangelism today must be loving, gentle, patient, and in some cases very slow. Some people may take the jump into God's love at events or on a Sunday morning through an experience of corporate worship; but I believe most will make the jump only after coming to trust a community of believers over time. It took time for the three-foot walls to be built, and it will take time to take the risk of that initial jump. This first jump into the Christian life is not easy. Maybe it was the same for Peter.

But this initial jump was not the only one that Peter had to make. The impala does not have the ability to jump only once in its life. The impala has the ability to jump over and over again, each time experiencing the liberation that it brings. Peter had many other occasions where he had to decide to jump.

The story is told of Peter and the rest of the disciples on a boat waiting for Jesus. Out of nowhere, Jesus approached them, walking on the water. Peter looked, wondering if it was truly

Jesus approaching them in this miraculous way. Jesus called to Peter to come out onto the water himself. Right there, Peter had a decision to make: Jump or don't jump. He had already made the initial jump to follow Jesus; now he had to decide whether to say yes to an invitation that most would say was impossible. It's one thing to follow a man; it's quite another to jump out of a boat and walk on water.

On another occasion, Jesus was presenting a hard teaching about His identity and the cost of following Him. Many people began to turn away. Peter was faced with another jumping opportunity:

> *As a result of this many of His disciples withdrew and were not walking with Him anymore. So Jesus said to the twelve, "You do not want to go away also, do you?" Simon Peter answered Him, "Lord, to whom shall we go? You have words of eternal life. We have believed and have come to know that You are the Holy One of God."*

> **John 6:66–69**

When given the opportunity to go to a deeper place of understanding with God, will you take the jump? Even if the teaching presents challenges and issues that seem impossible to take on in daily living? Jumping is seldom easy. Sometimes it even feels like the more you jump, the harder the next jump is.

About a year ago, I took a trip to El Salvador through a partnership with Compassion International and Kingdom Building Ministries. We visited many of the Compassion International projects that are run in partnership with local churches. As part of a team of itinerant speakers with Kingdom Building Ministries, I connect my messages on Kingdom laborship and advancement with the Kingdom values of compassion, justice, and mercy. The ministries of Compassion International that seek to advance God's Kingdom and deal with poverty through child sponsorship are a great expression of this.

On our last day in El Salvador, we went zip-lining. I had never zip-lined in my life, and I have to say that I was dealing with a lot of fear. One of the other itinerant speakers, Adrian Dupree, seemed really excited about the chance. I told him I wasn't going to do it, but he insisted: "Efrem, you need to face your fears." After a lot of prayer and encouragement from both Compassion International and Kingdom Building staff, I decided to take the jump.

Zip-lining is traveling down a cable while in the air from one point to another. It's like coming down a mountain on a ski-lift chair except there's no chair—it's just you, holding on to a cable rigging.

Our zip-lining adventure took us up in the mountains, four hundred feet above the ground. As we traveled up the mountain by truck, I became very nervous. I didn't know what was on the other side of this experience. We finally stopped to put on our gear and then hiked farther up the mountain to get to the proper elevation. Remember now, I was doing this for the first time.

The instructors gave us directions for zip-lining—how to go, how to slow down, and how to stop. They also showed us how to initially get ourselves hooked on to the cable that would take us down the mountain. To get attached, you literally jump up and connect to the cable. When I stopped thinking about how high up I was and focused more on jumping up and getting connected, facing my fears was a little easier. It didn't take away my fears, but it made it more manageable. Since I am a pastor, the spiritual comparisons were racing through my head. In our relationship with God, it's not just about making a jump; it's about trusting the One we're connected to, even though we can't always see the destination. The key is to abide in God through Christ and the indwelling of the Holy Spirit:

> *So Jesus was saying to those Jews who had believed Him, "If you continue in My word, then you are truly disciples of Mine; and you will know the truth, and the truth will make you free."*
>
> **John 8:31–32**

◆ ◆

I want to go back to Peter for a moment. As I look at his life and faith, I see three jumps that were defining for Peter. Even though the Christian life is made up of multiple jumps, these three were vital for Peter. I believe they are for you and me as well:

   1. The jump into the beloved self

     2. The jump into the beloved church

       3. The jump into the beloved world

The Beloved Self

Everything begins somewhere. For Peter, everything began when Jesus said, "Follow Me." I don't believe Peter understood all that invitation meant, but he made the decision to take that initial jump. From there he kept on following, even when many turned away. Peter's jump took him to a moment of denying Jesus (John 18:16–27), but that moment was later redeemed. The resurrected Christ made sure Peter knew His forgiveness and grace and love (John 21:15–17). Through time and trial, Peter learned what it means to be the beloved of God. What about you? Do you live like you believe God loves you?

The Beloved Church

The beloved self overflows into the beloved church. Peter began to see this when he preached on the day of Pentecost and became a leader in the first Christ-centered community. He had no idea where all this would lead.

What does it look like to live in community with others? I'm not talking about just showing up for church on Sunday but actually living the Christian life with others and being willing to be held accountable. Now that is a major jump!

I served as the senior pastor of a church that is intentionally evangelical, multicultural, and urban. This type of church is rare in the United States of America. Race and class still can be very challenging issues in our society, so for a church like this one to be healthy and missional takes people willing to make the jump to build relationships and trust with people who are different from them; in other words, jumping from "God loves me" to "God loves us." The three-foot walls in this case could be fear, ignorance, prejudice, and past hurts. Taking the jumps over the long haul to be a reconciling gathering is essential to being the beloved church.

The Beloved World

But it doesn't stop with the church. In Acts 11, Peter was given a vision that challenged him to jump further and higher into the beloved world. Peter had no idea where taking the gospel message to the Gentiles would land him, but he took the leap.

This jump is about understanding and acting on how God has uniquely designed us to advance His Kingdom; in other words, jumping from "God loves us" to "God so loved the world." It's about becoming a vehicle of compassion, mercy, justice, and truth.

My "beloved" language comes from the vision of civil rights leader and pastor Dr. Martin Luther King Jr., who spoke often of "the beloved community"—a community of peace, love, reconciliation, and justice. But the origin of the civil rights movement came not from the speeches of Dr. King but from the jump of a woman named Rosa Parks.

Ms. Parks refused to go to the back of a bus and give up the seat she was sitting in for a white person. She ignited a movement by taking that jump. She had no idea where it would land. There was something Rosa Parks believed in: that God loved her, regardless of what the segregated South thought at the time. Her jump was based on seeing herself beyond how she was seen by those of the dominant racial group. She took the jump into the new self, a self that could live equally with whites and have equal access to all open seats on a bus. She sat still and jumped into the pursuit of the beloved self.

Rosa Parks's courage spilled over into the churches. But the people needed a leader, someone to take the jump and organize and strategize for the many. Dr. Martin Luther King Jr. took that leap. His jump resulted in a movement that hit the streets through bus boycotts, lunch-counter sit-ins, and freedom marches. This was a going public, jumping into the beloved world, the very transforming of society.

Ms. Parks and Dr. King had no idea where their jumps would end. Dr. King's cost him his life. But our world is so much better for it. Every faith jump you take has a risk factor, including the possibility of losing your life in order to find that faith.

But think about the alternatives: A world full of African impalas behind three-foot walls. Fishermen invited to become something more but don't because they're afraid. Pastors who might never experience the thrill of a zip-line. Or men and women forced to the back of the bus or the back of living. Jumping is the difference between a limited life and a liberated life, between just getting by and going further and higher.

What about you—are you ready to jump?

Chapter 2

CONNECTION

I am the true vine, and My Father is the vinedresser. Every branch in Me that does not bear fruit, He takes away; and every branch that bears fruit, He prunes it so that it may bear more fruit.... Abide in Me, and I in you. As the branch cannot bear fruit of itself unless it abides in the vine, so neither can you unless you abide in Me.

John 15:1–2, 4

You are My friends if you do what I command you. No longer do I call you slaves, for the slave does not know

what his master is doing; but I have called you friends,
for all things that I have heard from My Father I have
made known to you.

John 15:14–15

God calls us to be laborers who advance His Kingdom on the earth from a foundation of intimacy and an overflowing life of transformation. Through Jesus Christ and the indwelling of the Holy Spirit, we are friends with almighty God, given a life of purpose and mission. This kind of living is our on-ramp to the beloved life. When you have a community of people who are walking in intimate relationship with God in this way, with a heart-sense of Kingdom mission, you have the ingredients for a beloved church. A beloved church has one goal: advancing the Kingdom of God through *laborship*. Laborship is a liberating, mission-filled movement in which God's beloved followers combine their resources of time, talents, and treasure to bring the compassion, mercy, truth, justice, and transformation of God into the world. It takes a willingness to jump over the wall of religion and institutionalism in order to become this kind of church. But even before that, it takes individuals making the choice to jump over the wall of a Christian life of individualism.

The beloved life begins by looking beyond how the Christian life benefits us to how God desires to use us to advance Him and His Kingdom. Some can't make this jump because they have the wrong perspective on how God sees them and the kind of intimate relationship that God wants with His children. Some go to church every Sunday hoping to get something from God to get through the week, not realizing that God wants to *be* their week by being intimately connected to them daily. The wrong views on God and the Christian life can actually become the three-foot wall that keeps us from the liberating journey of living in the beloved self—this daily, intimate relationship with God. It's all rooted in the belief that through Jesus Christ, God is well pleased with me.

But how do I know that God is well pleased with me? I know that the Father is well pleased with the Son, Jesus Christ. And if Christ lives in me through the Holy Spirit, then I become the one in whom God is well pleased! This becomes my identity. God loved me, as a human being in the world, so much that thousands of years before I was born, He sent His Son, Jesus, into the world so that years later I would accept Him into my life as Lord and Savior. Through this faith jump of believing that He is the Son of God who died on the cross for me and rose from the grave, my life is transformed. My old self passes away, and now I live the life of the beloved self, which is the starting point of the beloved life. I say starting point because the Christian life doesn't end with making the faith jump into the love of God.

This initial jump is in some supernatural way like jumping into the loving arms of God. God pursues us with His love, and we jump into that pursuit. This reminds me of when I was a little boy, getting ready for bed. I would go into my room, put my pajamas on, and run into the front room to say good night to my mother and father. My mother sat on a couch that was low to the floor, so when I said good night to her, it was like falling into her arms. But my dad sat in his own chair that was higher off the floor. I remember taking somewhat of a running start and then jumping into his arms. He would hug me and kiss me and tell me good night.

I recall other men in my family and jumping into their arms and their love for me as well. I had a great-uncle on my father's side I called Uncle Wes. Uncle Wes always had money for my younger brother and me, but the money was not the main reason I ran to him (though I'm not complaining about that). I ran into his arms because I sensed his love for me. My Uncle Wes was a big, tall man, and to reach his arms when he was standing I had to jump really high. He would usually meet me halfway by bending down. He had a thick beard that would scratch my face when I hugged him. Then there was a great-uncle on my mother's side named Jay. When he would come over, he would always give my younger brother and me a hug and a kiss on the forehead. I could keep going, but what I'm trying to point out here is that I was very fortunate growing up to have men in my family who poured out great love for me.

Even today as an adult, I still feel warm inside when I think about jumping into their arms and experiencing their love for me. My dad, uncles, and grandfathers were such strong symbols of love that when I finally made the decision to jump into the love of my heavenly Father by accepting Christ as my Lord and Savior, it wasn't a huge hurdle. I already had a frame of reference from a family of loving men. I can only imagine that boys who don't grow up with loving men in their family have a hard time seeing the Christian life as jumping into the arms of a loving heavenly Father.

I remember meeting a high school boy who was referred to me by his guidance counselor. The counselor had told me that the boy had recently moved to Minneapolis from Chicago. She believed he was a bright and gifted young man, but recently he had started acting angrily and wasn't doing well in school. She thought that because I had a reputation of working with young men as a former high school basketball coach and youth minister that maybe I could have some sort of impact in his life. I met with him over lunch at the school one day. My first impressions were the same as what the counselor had told me—smart, talented kid. As we ate, he explained his move from Chicago to Minneapolis with his mother and father. He said that since they had arrived, his parents seemed to argue and fight all the time. One day his father took him out to one of his favorite places to eat. He told him that he had had another fight with his mother and that they had decided to split up. And to top it off, the boy found out this man wasn't his real father. After telling the boy this news, he pulled out a box with a brand-new pair of shoes and explained to the boy that this would be the last gift he would receive from him because after all, "I'm not your real father." The boy looked at me and said, "I think that's when my problems began."

It took a lot for me to hold back tears after this. He said that though he was hurt and angry, he was planning to go back to Chicago as soon as the school year ended to try to find his real father. I tried to talk to him that day about God's love for him even if he didn't find his real father. I talked to him about the church he attended with his mother and possibly connecting with godly men there. I knew the pastor at the church he attended and felt I could help connect him, but I could tell that through the pain of losing a father's love, a three-foot wall now surrounded him. I was doing all I knew how to convince him to jump.

I realize there are many people who have grown up with painful experiences that build walls, making it harder to say yes and jump into God's love for them. This is why those of us who have made the jump cannot keep this freedom to ourselves. We must reach out to others and lovingly call them to make the leap themselves. As an adult man, I realize the need to pour into the lives of boys, especially those who didn't grow up in an environment full of loving men with arms wide open.

Seeing God as a loving Father was not a three-foot wall for me. This is not to say that I didn't have my own obstacles to deal with though. I definitely did. My initial wall had to do with growing up in church and getting beyond attendance and activity alone to an intimate relationship with God through Jesus Christ. I was in church, but I needed to make the jump into the beloved self. I had said yes to the relationship with God; now I needed to abide in Him.

◆ ◆

A church community who had a sense of mission and transformation influenced my life at an early age. I can truly say it was a beloved church. Tabernacle Missionary Baptist Church was a small African

American congregation located on the south side of Minneapolis. Though they didn't have the resources to hire a youth pastor, they had a sense of mission to the surrounding community by reaching out to young people like me. They created an alternative social event called Friday Night—a dance party put on in the church on the first Friday of every month. I remember being invited by my friend Stewart. I couldn't believe what I saw when I entered the church! There was hip-hop music playing, lights flashing, and the smell of southern soul food! All this in a Baptist church, mind you. You paid a couple of dollars to get in. (I know what you're thinking: *A cover charge to get in church?*) I received a ticket when I went in and was directed to the fellowship hall, where the ticket was turned in for a chicken dinner and red Kool-Aid. I love red Kool-Aid to this day because of that experience.

There were older adults, deacons, and mothers of the church in the kitchen serving the food and making sure we had a good time. It was one of the best parties I ever went to as a kid, and more importantly, it was my entry into the broader life of the church. This congregation was a beloved church, on a mission to transform the lives of young people. It would be years later before my life would be more deeply transformed, but it started by being connected to the church, which is not in any way a bad thing. This initial involvement in church, through that youth dance party, pulled me into some very positive activities. I became involved in youth choir, Sunday school, and the youth usher board. I made the jump into church, a good step toward an intimate relationship with Christ. After a while I was baptized and became a member of this church. From the sixth grade to my first year in high school, this beloved church cared for and challenged my relationship with Christ.

As deep as that connection can be, it is not as powerful as the supernatural connection to God's love. Eventually I lost my connection to the church. My mother served as one of the choir directors and during a choir rehearsal got into an argument with the senior pastor. I'm not sure what it was about; I just remember that we stopped going to church. To be honest, once we stopped going, I really didn't miss it all that much; I just started connecting to other things and other people. I connected to the boys I played football with and other kids in my neighborhood. Church was something I connected to because my mother and grandmother were involved with it. The youth activities were an initial draw and kept my interest, but once my mother and grandmother stopped attending and that connection was severed, I simply stopped going to church and just moved on to the next thing. I was a good kid, but my church connection had not led to a spiritually transformed life. This was a jump I would take later.

I transferred to a new high school my sophomore year—Minneapolis North High School. It was there I met a kid named Joey. He talked to me about his church all the time, but I wasn't really moved by this because I knew what it meant to be connected to the church. What really moved me was that Joey talked a lot about his relationship with Jesus. Joey didn't talk about Jesus only to me; he shared the Lord with just about every other kid on the bus to and from school as well as the ones who sat with us in the cafeteria during lunch. As I write this, I can see in my mind Joey trying to tell as many kids about his relationship with Jesus as he could. I was intrigued by this because I don't remember Joey really inviting me to church even though he talked about his church and even introduced me to Bart, his youth director. Like I said, what Joey talked a lot about was Jesus.

During the summer before the next school year, I connected with Joey's church—Park Avenue United Methodist Church. While there, I accepted Jesus Christ as my Lord and Savior. My life was transformed, and I eventually jumped into the beloved life. I jumped over the three-foot wall of superficial church association to being deeply connected to God through Jesus Christ and the indwelling of the Holy Spirit.

I connected to the church that summer, but it was at a high school weekend retreat during my junior year when I became a Christian. At that retreat, a speaker named Buster preached a sermon on agape love—the unconditional love of God toward us. Even though I had heard a lot of sermons about God, this one focused on God's love for me. Although there were many other youth in that multipurpose room, it felt as if only three people were there—Buster, God, and me. I stood up at the conclusion of the sermon, walked forward, and jumped into the arms of God's love. I have to admit it felt so much bigger than jumping into the arms of my dad, Uncle Wes, or Uncle Jay. I took the jump into a personal relationship with God through Jesus Christ, but this was just the beginning. After this initial leap over the wall of church connection, I was encouraged to take yet another jump.

Joey invited me to join him in sharing the love of God with others we knew in high school. He talked to me about his relationship with Bart, the high school youth director at the time, and the impact he was having on his life. Through being discipled by Bart, Joey had lovingly befriended me and another kid, named Julian, with the purpose of introducing us to the beloved life. Because of these loving and missional relationships, both of us had become Christians.

Bart began meeting each week with the three of us. We met for a Bible study that focused on an intimate relationship with God, sharing Jesus with others, and living a life of compassion, mercy, and justice. As a result of this experience as a teenager some things began to come together for me that were very important in connecting what I now call the beloved self, the beloved church, and the beloved world.

Through a focus on an intimate relationship with God, I learned that my spiritual life could be so much bigger than just a connection to church. My initial connection to church was very important and had a tremendous impact on my life, but now I was gaining an understanding that I could have a daily connection to God, one that could be deep and real. Although this was an invisible relationship, I could sense the connection on the inside as I studied the Word and spent time in prayer. It was wonderful and mysterious, yet I could feel the connection—God loves me, and it was real!

I also learned through the weekly Bible studies that the Christian life is not to be lived in isolation but rather lived out in community. I then understood the importance of a connection to the church: the support of friends who also had a desire to grow in Christ. We held each other accountable. I remember when I started dating a girl who wasn't a Christian, how Joey and Julian shared their concerns with me. I remember Bart taking me out to my favorite burger place and sharing his heart with me as well. This care by Christian brothers and sisters is what the beloved church is all about: praying together and spending time in the Word together. This is the challenge for churches today. The church must be more than a weekend worship service or some kind of religious country club. It must be a place where people form reconciling relationships out of the overflow of being reconciled to God.

I didn't make this jump in my first connection to church. My initial church experience in some ways was very cultural. As an African American, I connected to an African American church, which had ministries and preached sermons that were relevant to African American culture. I'm not criticizing this in any way, and I understand the need for a church geared specifically toward African Americans and their spiritual development and empowerment in a predominantly European American society. But my initial connection was a cultural one, one that did not lead me to grow deeply in an intimate relationship with Christ. I believe this is one of the potential problems with the church in black and white; it can drift to become culture centered rather than Christ centered.

But my experience at Park Avenue Methodist was different; it was multicultural. The fact that the youth ministry was multicultural caused no one culture to dominate and be the center. Christ is always the center in a multicultural church community. This to me is what made it a beloved church. My discipleship experience was multicultural because Bart was European American, Joey was Native American, and Julian and I were African American. What I liked about Bart's discipleship style was that he wasn't trying to make us white; he was trying to draw us into a deep relationship with Christ and into community with each other as well as others within the youth group.

◆ ◆

One of the pivotal lessons I learned in this multicultural church was that God desires to use us to advance His Kingdom. Bart talked to us a lot about sharing God's love with others. He also talked about compassion, mercy, and justice. We talked about poverty in third world countries and God's heart as revealed in Scripture to do something about it. This was the beginning of my understanding and making the jump into advancing the beloved world, and this jump is about becoming God's vehicle for redemption within His creation. Equipped with this understanding, we shared God's love with others at school and saw many come to Christ.

We started an ethnically diverse, student-led Bible study at school that grew to close to one hundred students. This became a beloved church of sorts right there on campus. I began to really develop a passion for racial reconciliation and justice. Joey, Julian, and I started a band called Brothers in Christ. Both Joey and Julian could play keyboards really well, and we all sang. We recruited a kid named Charles to play drums and another one named Doug to strengthen the vocals. We played at talent shows, local gospel concerts, and outreach events. I remember playing at a community event aimed toward bringing peace between rival gangs in our neighborhood. Joey wrote a song called "Agape Love," which shared how we made the jump into God's love for us and our desire to share it with others. We were singing about Jesus to gang members, and some of those men gave their lives to Christ that night. As teenagers, we had become vehicles of God's love and transformation in our own community. I share this story because it gives a picture of those who make the jump beyond church attendance and an individual relationship with God to a life of transformation. This is the beloved life, connecting the beloved self, the beloved church, and the beloved world. We must consider where we are in our spiritual lives and ask ourselves, *Is it time to make yet another jump?*

Do you need to jump beyond living life in your own power? Do you need to jump beyond simply attending church or participating in church activities? Do you need to jump into the arms of our loving Savior? Do you need to jump into the life of advancing God's Kingdom by saying yes to His plan for transformation?

In the fifteenth chapter of the gospel of John, the words of Jesus to His followers provide a practical theology for what His plan of transformation looks like in our lives. Jesus begins the chapter by stating that He is the true vine and His Father is the vinedresser. We are later described as a branch connected to the vine. Because Jesus the Son and God the Father are one, we see something powerful in the context of being transformed by God and living a life of transformation in the world. Because God is both the vine and the vinedresser, simultaneously we are connected to God and we are cared for by God. We grow in the life of the beloved self by allowing God to care for us, as we stay connected to Him. The Bible uses the word *abide,* meaning to dwell, to stay, to say, "God, I'm not going anywhere." The beloved self is about a surrendering, a dying to being in control of ourselves and trusting the One who makes us the beloved. In this experience we come to believe that God's care for us is better than our own. Through God the vinedresser we are loved; through God the vine we stay connected in God's love.

The purpose of the branch on the vine is to bear fruit. If the branch does not bear fruit, it is void of Kingdom purpose and is useless. This is where the phrase "heaven bound, but no earthly good" comes into play. Bearing fruit, or Kingdom advancement, is the life of one who is liberated and empowered by God. As liberated, beloved beings, we become vehicles of compassion, mercy, justice, truth, and transformation in the world. This work leads to people coming to Christ, which is of utmost importance, but it also leads to Kingdom acts of justice, dealing head-on with poverty, racism, sexism, hunger, and the need for health care. Injustice is a demonic force. We do not have it within ourselves to deal with that which is ultimately rooted in principalities. But by being connected to the vine and cared for by God, we become spiritual power brokers who bring true love and justice into the world. This is what God does through us.

In John 15:3, Jesus says, "You are already clean because of the word which I have spoken to you." Jesus' comment is about what God does in us. We are made clean through Christ Jesus. Failing to understand this becomes a three-foot wall standing between us and our participation in the world. If we don't believe we are clean, we can feel unworthy of advancing God's Kingdom. It is the paralyzing power of shame. Sometimes preachers can actually participate in this shaming, telling believers how much they've fallen short instead of equipping them to be Kingdom advancers. This is not to downplay the importance of righteous living, but it is to provide the balance of grace as well as to emphasize that righteousness comes by staying connected. It hurts my heart as a pastor that I meet so many people who are caged by shame, a three-foot wall keeping many who believe in God from being vehicles of His love to others.

Even the pruning that is mentioned in verse 2 is about the work God is doing within us so that He might produce fruit through us. Pruning should not be seen as a shaming process or some kind of punishment from God. The pruning is about our further maturity and development in the beloved life. This is true because God is not physically pruning us, as a human vinedresser would do with actual branches on a vine. The pruning of God is about our spiritual formation that takes place on the inside of our being, the "soul work" that we must allow God to do in us through the Holy Spirit. This is the work that must take place in order for us to truly be kind, gentle, patient, and unselfish.

As John 15 continues, Jesus says that if we abide in Him, He abides in us, and we will bear much fruit. So our intimacy with God bears out much purpose and transformation in the world. Don't underestimate the Kingdom impact you can make in your family, community, school, or at work. Your intimate relationship with God can lead to great things. God is in the business of using ordinary people to do extraordinary things. God can use you to lead a gang member to Christ, as my friends and I did as teenagers. God can use you to speak reconciliation into a marriage on the verge of divorce. God can use you to speak life to someone considering suicide. I know this may seem like an overwhelming task, but it's all possible when you're abiding in the vine.

I love what Jesus says in verse 15: "No longer do I call you slaves, for the slave does not know what his master is doing; but I have called you friends, for all things that I have heard from My Father I have made known to you."

The context of slavery here points to indentured servitude. This is a type of slavery that is about paying off a debt. Sin put humanity in debt to God. But God, in His overwhelming love for us, sent His own Son, Jesus Christ, to pay this debt on our behalf. Now that the debt has been paid, our identity has been transformed from slave to friend. God's love transforms our being from the inside that we might bear fruit on the outside. Our job is to abide in the vine, so through that foundation of intimacy we become agents of Kingdom transformation in the world.

This biblical understanding has become pivotal for me as I speak around the country on the issues of justice and reconciliation. In our ever-increasing multiethnic and multicultural world the word *reconciliation* is very relevant. I've been preaching for a number of years on reconciliation in the context of unity within the body of Christ across race and ethnicity. But as I've grown deeper in my understanding of abiding in the vine, I've learned that reconciliation must also be dealt with as a word that speaks to spiritual formation as well. We cannot truly be reconciled to each other without understanding the reality and depth to which we are reconciled to God through Jesus Christ and the indwelling of the Holy Spirit. We must have a holistic understanding of reconciliation so that it might point us toward intimacy with God as well as becoming an outer force of transformation that tears down walls of division, no matter what height, in our world.

Chapter 3

BELOVED

Beloved, let us love one another, for love is from God; and everyone who loves is born of God and knows God. The one who does not love does not know God, for God is love. By this the love of God was manifested in us, that God has sent His only begotten Son into the world so that we might live through Him.

1 John 4:7–9

I decided a couple of years ago that every January, as it came close to the Dr. Martin Luther King Jr. national holiday, I would spend time reading some of his essential speeches and writings. Each year through this experience I find myself drawn to Dr. King's focus on the beloved community. As I read about his vision and strategy during the civil rights movement, it was clear to me that the love of God shown through Jesus Christ played a major role. Nonviolence was the strategy, but the beloved community was the vision. Nonviolence was the vehicle through which love was used to take on the hate that fueled racial segregation and racism. I saw this clearly in his writing "An Experiment in Love," which focuses on the power of agape love.

> *From the beginning a basic philosophy guided the movement. This guiding principle has since been referred to variously as nonviolent resistance, noncooperation, and passive resistance. But in the first days of the protest none of these expressions was mentioned: the phrase most often heard was "Christian love." … It was Jesus of Nazareth that stirred the Negroes to protest with the creative weapon of love.*
>
> **Page 16, *A Testament of Hope: The Essential Writings and Speeches of Martin Luther King Jr.*, edited by James M. Washington**

Nonviolent resistance had emerged as the technique of the movement, while love stood as the regulating ideal. In other words, Christ furnished the spirit and motivation, while Gandhi furnished the method.

Page 17, *A Testament of Hope*

When we speak of loving those who oppose us, we refer to neither eros *nor* philia; *we speak of a love which is expressed in the Greek word* agape.... *It is the love of God operating in the human heart.*

Page 19, *A Testament of Hope*

These words of Dr. King led me to consider that the love of God that transforms our lives is able to flow through us so we might have an impact on the sins of injustice surrounding us. We can be light in the darkness; we can be the salt of the earth merely by being willing to abide in God's love. As we stay in God's love, our lives become the very vehicles God uses to forge the beloved community. We live out of the overflow of God's love, and the redemption and reconciliation that we experience through Christ is extended to others, even our enemies. Dr. King drew a sharp contrast between the one living in love and the one living in hate:

The nonviolent resister must often express his protest through noncooperation or boycotts, but he realizes that

these are not ends themselves.... The end is redemption
and reconciliation. The aftermath of nonviolence
is the creation of the beloved community, while the
aftermath of violence is tragic bitterness.

Page 18, *A Testament of Hope*

As I have deeply considered Dr. King's vision for the beloved community, the civil rights movement has become more to me than merely a political or protest movement. It has become a Kingdom-advancing movement, ignited by men and women, boys and girls connected to God and local churches. They took the jump beyond the wall of mere church attendance and membership and allowed the love of God to become a weapon for justice through them.

The beloved community becomes the beloved world when we make the connection that the overflow of God's love for transformation is bigger than any national social movement. With this in mind, I am now convinced that there can be no beloved world without a beloved church, and there can be no beloved church without beloved beings living daily in beloved selves. A movement of Kingdom transformation begins with first taking the jump into the amazing love of God. In 1 John, we find foundational writing on the love, of which Dr. King speaks, that was the center of the civil rights movement.

Beloved, let us love one another, for love is from God;
and everyone who loves is born of God and knows God.

1 John 4:7

Though the amazing love of God can ignite a movement of Kingdom transformation, it must first be a transformational force in the life of an individual. Before a beloved church or a beloved world can exist, there must first be the beloved self. In 1 John 4, two words in the Greek are being used to give us an understanding of how God desires to root His amazing love within us, and then also to create an overflow that causes us to become a force of love in the world. In 1 John 4:7, John says that we ought to love one another and that this love is from God. This type of love is represented by the Greek word *agapao*. This word means to love and to be loved. The understanding here is that we cannot truly love one another as God desires us to without first living in God's love. Loving someone else ought to be an overflow of our love relationship with God. We must be willing to jump into God's love for us and then allow the force of that love to empower us to jump into righteous, loving relationships with others.

Within the civil rights movement, which to a certain degree was a Kingdom-advancing movement, it took a love that could only come from God to love those who would beat you, sic dogs on you, and turn fire hoses on you simply for marching for freedom and sitting at segregated lunch counters. It takes an amazing love to love those who hate you for pursuing equality. Beloved beings who live in intimate relationship with God through the power of the Holy Spirit have the ability to live in community as the beloved church and become a force of transformation to create the beloved world.

◆ ◆

The second word for love used in 1 John 4:7 talks about this love from God, which transforms us into the beloved self. This word for love in the Greek is *agape*—the benevolent love of God that we do not deserve but that is offered to us by Him anyhow. This benevolent, compassionate, and merciful love of God transforms our lives so that we become beloved beings. But beloved beings can't keep this amazing love to ourselves. This incredible love is so powerful that we can't contain it. When we make the jump into God's love and live in it daily, it ought to affect those around us. We are loved and loving simultaneously. But this is no ordinary love. This is not just a love that causes you to love those who are like you but a love that causes you to love your enemies. It's a love that causes you to become a radical reconciler.

God's love is a reconciling love because it goes after the one who has sinned against God. God's love offers life to the one who deserves death. To this degree, it's a radical reconciling love: God is a reconciler, and Jesus Christ is the vehicle for reconciliation. Through the crucifixion and resurrection of Christ, reconciliation between God and man is made possible. When people jump into this reconciling love, they are then empowered through the overflow of this love to become a reconciler. This reconciling love not only equips us to live in community with other beloved beings in order to become the beloved church, but it also empowers us to become vehicles of compassion, mercy, and justice. We are able to love our enemies. We are able to reconcile broken relationships. Reconciliation is a vital act of one living in the beloved life.

As we read further in 1 John 4, we see that it is through the reconciler, Jesus Christ, that we receive this love:

By this the love of God was manifested in us, that God has sent His only begotten Son into the world so that we might live through Him. In this is love, not that we loved God, but that He loved us and sent His Son to be the propitiation for our sins.

1 John 4:9–10

My life as a Christian must exhibit the life of one living in intimacy with God through Jesus Christ and the indwelling of the Holy Spirit. The vital question for Christians ought to be "Are we loving?" instead of "How well do we pray?" "How many Scriptures have we memorized?" or "How many days have we fasted?" Not that these things are unimportant, but love is key. Consider the words of Paul in 1 Corinthians 13:

If I speak with the tongues of men and of angels, but do not have love, I have become a noisy gong or a clanging cymbal. If I have the gift of prophecy, and know all mysteries and all knowledge; and if I have all faith, so as to remove mountains, but do not have love, I am nothing. And if I give all my possessions to feed the poor, and if I surrender my body to be burned, but do not have love, it profits me nothing.

1 Corinthians 13:1–3

This type of love is expressed best through Jesus Christ, and it ignites the possibility of living as the beloved self. It's one thing to jump into the God-loving pursuit of us by accepting Jesus Christ as our Lord and Savior. We must also be willing to take the jump to live daily in this love. This jump is about living daily "in the know" that God loves us.

> *We have come to know and have believed the love which God has for us. God is love, and the one who abides in love abides in God, and God abides in him.*
>
> **1 John 4:16**

◆ ◆

As a young person in middle school, I made the jump into church. As a teenager in high school, I made the jump into God's love for me by accepting Jesus Christ as my Lord and Savior. I still had another jump to make though: a jump into understanding the need to abide in God's love for me daily and living daily in the knowledge that God loves me, even when I don't feel it.

The next jump I realized I needed to make came during my junior year in college. However, it took me three years to make this jump because my problem actually began my freshman year. I graduated from Minneapolis North High School. This is an urban public high school, which at the time I graduated was about 70 percent African American; I was a member of the majority at North High. I attended college at Saint John's University in central Minnesota. This is an all-male Catholic university that is coed academically through a partnership with the College of Saint Benedict, a Catholic school for women. At the time the schools combined had an enrollment of about 3,600. My freshman year I was one of seven African American students on the whole campus. This was an incredibly hard transition for me culturally, and by the end of my first year I was seriously considering a transfer. One of the reasons I stayed was because of my father. One, I was committed to stay in college in general because I realized how hard he and my mother were working to support me financially. Two, I can still remember sitting down with my dad and listening to him encourage me not to give up just because it was hard. Once again my father's love was probably an on-ramp to understanding God's love for me in the midst of my struggle in being at Saint John's. It would take me longer this time, though, to make the jump into abiding in God's love.

At Saint John's, my struggle was not just being in the vast minority on campus, but it was also receiving comments from the majority students as well as experiencing actions from some of them. One student told me that I was the first live black person he'd seen. This same person said that they had no blacks in the town where he had grown up and that he'd only seen black people on television until seeing me. It was assumed by many that I was a great basketball player and dancer (I wish I was making this up). Because a few miles separated the College of Saint Benedict and Saint John's University, there was a shuttle bus that took students back and forth to each campus for classes. Sometimes white students would sit three to a seat before they would sit with me. I sat in classes and would catch some white students just staring at me. This was very hard for me, and I know I internalized this to the point that I felt like an alien on campus, less than human.

I remember going into what is called the Great Hall at Saint John's University to pray because I was struggling so much. The Great Hall was the church on campus before the new abbey was constructed. As I sat there, I looked up to see a large mural of sorts depicting Jesus. As in most paintings, Jesus was white. This didn't help my struggle; in fact, at that moment it made it worse. I felt like an alien before the predominantly white student body and now was beginning to feel the same way before a white Jesus. I didn't sense God's agape love for me at that moment, and as I rose and walked back to my dorm room, I began to live differently on campus. I was angry, I was depressed, and I felt void of love. I felt less than human sitting alone on a packed campus shuttle bus and seeing some people choose to stand up in the back or sit three to a seat rather than sit with me. I began to hang out with just the few other black students on campus, and I stopped pursuing deeper growth as a Christian. Thankfully, God didn't stop pursuing me.

I realize now that I was broken on the inside. Brokenness can be another three-foot wall keeping us from understanding who we really are in Christ, as well as God's purpose for our lives in the world. Brokenness limits our ability to see more fully who we are as God's beloved. Let me say right now that I'm not using the metaphor of jumping to imply some sort of works righteousness. We are not jumping to gain God's love. Jumping is more a picture of realizing that liberation, love, and empowerment are just a jump away, readily available to us. They are available to us just by simply using the gifts that God has placed in us to respond to what He has already done for us. Through Christ Jesus, we have the ability to experience God's great love each day. God not only empowers us to jump into this love; He is coaxing us, calling us to jump. Again, as I described in the previous chapter, I see God as a loving Father with his arms open wide, calling us to jump. As I picture my own dad, I think of when I was a little kid and he would stand at the bottom of the stairs from my bedroom, calling me to jump into his arms. I would feel his love, but I was still somewhat scared to make the leap. The things around me influenced my willingness to just jump. This in no way took away from my father's love or his power to catch me and keep me from harm. Yet with all his love and ability, I let things around me, like the stairs between me and his open arms, cause me to question if I could jump or not.

Things around us, especially how we're treated by others, can create a three-foot wall that causes us to question the reality of God's love right in front of us. Remember, the African impala won't jump if it can't see where it will land. I was at Saint John's University not sure where I would land if I made the decision to stay there in the midst of feeling like a brother from another planet. But I soon realized that the issue was bigger than *Will I stay?* and was really about *Why did God put me here?* Could it be that you are where you are because God placed you there, as hard as that place may be? If this is true, you have to push past how you're being treated and do what God has placed you to do.

◆ ◆

Let's go back to the civil rights movement for a minute. African Americans were being treated unfairly because of the color of their skin. This racism was a societal three-foot wall of discrimination. Now when facing this situation, they had to decide if they would jump or not. Some may argue with me and say that racism is much bigger than a three-foot wall. Well, in our own power that may be very true; but to God, racism is just a three-foot wall, and when empowered by God's love, we have the ability to not only jump over this wall but also dismantle it so that for others, those who come behind us, the wall is not as high.

Now there were multiple ways that African Americans and others could respond to racism and discrimination during that time. One, they could just allow themselves to be socialized into how the dominant group saw them. They could live their lives as less than fully human, undeserving of equality with the majority. Another response was to ignite an angry rebellion, taking an eye-for-an-eye or a tooth-for-a-tooth approach. This is centered in revenge and doing unto others what they've done unto you. Neither one of these is the approach of one living in the beloved life.

In the beloved life, God's love ought to reign in and through our lives. To assimilate into second-class citizenship is to live below who we are as those made in the image of God. To live the life of revenge is to deny that God's love is a reconciling love. Remember, Jesus did not say do unto others as they've done unto you, but do unto others as you would have them (or want them) to do unto you. And what would I want them to do to me? Extend love. But what kind? Agape love.

As I said, as a freshman in college at Saint John's University I was not feeling like a beloved child of God. I'm not saying that the white students on campus hated me; I believe more that pure ignorance and a lack of cross-cultural relationship led to how I was being treated by some. In fact, some whites treated me very well, but I was so overwhelmed and downcast by those who didn't that many times I didn't acknowledge those who were truly trying to extend love and community to me. I saw people sitting three to a seat rather than sitting next to me more than I saw the white student who would sit next to me in class and try to start a conversation. I made the bus-seating situation the norm of white treatment rather than the classroom example. All of this combined with the white Jesus staring down at me in the Great Hall made me feel horrible and less than loved by God.

So many people allow treatment from others to affect their thoughts on how God feels about them. This is the switch that I needed to make. I was letting the treatment by some whites on campus and a man-made picture of a white Jesus cause me to question God's feelings about me. What should happen instead is that the biblical reality of God's love for me should influence how I respond to people, including people who don't treat me so well. This is the key to the jump I made over the three-foot wall I was facing in college. And it started in the campus library, of all places.

One of the ways I began to cope with what I was dealing with on campus was to schedule my classes as early as possible in the day and then spend the afternoon studying alone in the basement of the library, avoiding people. I just wanted to be left alone in my growing depression. This shows that it's possible to be in church, be a Christian, and be unhealthy based on a bad belief system.

As I stood at the front desk of the library one afternoon I noticed a documentary called *Eyes on the Prize* that was available in the video catalog. When I read more, I found out that this film dealt with the civil rights movement. I decided to check it out and go to the back of the library where there were televisions, video machines, and headphones. I started watching part one of a five-part video that day. I was so moved by watching the story of how a group of people responded to hate with love under the leadership of Dr. Martin Luther King Jr. that I was led to tears. The whole video was not about Dr. King's approach. The assimilation and revenge approaches were shown as well. Through my tears, I was forced to choose which approach I was going to take in dealing with what I was facing on campus. Would I assimilate into being the alien on campus? Would I seek revenge by treating white students the way that some were treating me? Would I become a force of love on campus? The tougher question, at least for me, was how does my choice connect to my being a Christian? That last question led me to connect the video with prayer and God's Word. The following words from Jesus in Matthew 5 began to give me some clarity:

> *You have heard that it was said, "An eye for an eye, and a tooth for a tooth." But I say to you, do not resist an evil person; but whoever slaps you on your right cheek, turn the other to him also. If anyone wants to sue you and take your shirt, let him have your coat also. Whoever forces you to go one mile, go with him two. Give to him who asks of you, and do not turn away from him who wants to borrow from you. You have heard that it was said, "You shall love your neighbor and hate your enemy." But I say to you, love your enemies and pray for those who persecute you, so that you may be sons of your Father who is in heaven.*

Matthew 5:38–45

These words of Jesus as interpreted by Dr. Martin Luther King Jr. fueled his approach to dealing with racism and discrimination against blacks in the 1950s and '60s. Jesus is the author of the blueprint for how to deal with enemies, a plan that carries the purpose of the transformation of the enemy. The weapon for dealing with enemies is love. This gave Dr. King his perspective on the civil rights movement and is also what led to his stance on the Vietnam

War. He saw love as the weapon of choice for the Christian in every battle. I took this notion and began to wrestle with what this meant for me as a Christian on the campus of Saint John's University. It was obvious to me that church membership and accepting Jesus Christ as my personal Savior were not enough. I had to take the jump into my true identity in Christ and what that meant for how I would respond to a challenging situation. I needed to jump into the daily life of the beloved self.

The beloved self is about identity. My entire self should be rooted in my identity in Christ. This was an important jump for me. My identity is not shaped by the majority culture; it's shaped by God. We see this in 1 John 3:

> *See how great a love the Father has bestowed on us, that we would be called children of God; and such we are.*
>
> **1 John 3:1**

◆ ◆

Our identity is shaped by God's love, not by people around us. This I believe has been the force of transformation for African Americans in the United States, who for the most part have found liberation through strategies that came out of the black church. Also, it must be noted that others with the white church and other faith communities joined in on this journey of social transformation. To this degree and through the civil rights movement we are able to see beloved individuals coming into community as the beloved church to forge a movement to realize a beloved world. Many evangelicals have not been able to see the significance of this because they see the civil rights movement only as a social gospel movement. Some don't even see a gospel (good news) movement at all and have relegated it to a political movement of sorts. The civil rights movement ought to be seen as a revival and renewal movement fueled by the deeds and words of Christ.

What did all this mean for me on the campus of Saint John's University in the early 1990s? I began to find deeper freedom and identity through studying God's Word to find out more of who I was in Him. I began to smile at people who wouldn't sit next to me on the bus because I realized more and more that if they sat next to me or not, it didn't take away from who I was. The next step God led me to was to give those who were ignorant of me a more Christ-centered and authentic picture of myself. With a multiethnic group of students, we formed the Coalition for Black Cultural Awareness. This group was not a separatist, all-black group but a group committed to educating the whole campus on the richness of African American culture in order to help Saint John's become a truly multicultural campus. We put on movie nights, forums, and parties, which featured foods from African American culture. We were surprised by the tremendous turnout at the events. I also began to write for the student newspaper for both Saint John's University and the College of Saint Benedict. I soon had my own column in the Saint Benedict paper called "A New Movement." I really began to enjoy my time on campus because I found purpose out of who I truly was in Christ, not based on how people who lacked knowledge of African Americans saw me. It wasn't just about a desire for people to know who I was as an African American, which was important, but also who I was as a Christian.

I also began using my talents in theater and music to create a beloved community on campus. I used my talent of singing to put on gospel concerts in coffeehouses, where I shared my testimony of how I became a Christian. For a project as a theater major I also partnered with a white student named Joe Rux to perform a two-man play called *Blot Knot*, which dealt with issues of justice and reconciliation in South Africa during apartheid. During my junior year, I even ran for student government and was successful in winning my campaign and serving the student body. I went from an alien to a campus leader by taking the jump into the beloved self. This is not to say that I didn't struggle from time to time. Lord knows I did. The key is I was able to deal with the ignorance and even racism on campus by understanding more of the power of God's love in transforming my identity and giving me purpose in the midst of pain.

Years later, after I graduated from Saint John's, I was invited back to speak at the senior banquet about my time on campus. I'm so glad I didn't transfer, because even today that experience impacts my call to live a life that advances God's Kingdom. When I was the pastor at the multicultural Sanctuary Covenant Church, I realized that my experience at Saint John's of jumping over the three-foot walls of brokenness and separations put in place through a race-based society had allowed me to see that other part of the beloved life. My brokenness was replaced with a greater sense of being the beloved child of God and positioned me for a calling of advancing the beloved world through leading a reconciling movement. Identity in the beloved self is a discipline and journey, which allows us to move from brokenness to purpose. I found a sense of purpose at Saint John's University that gave me a greater sense of freedom in Christ and a place in the advancement of God's Kingdom.

Chapter 4

HEAVEN

I'll never forget riding my bike past Park Avenue United Methodist Church in south Minneapolis and seeing something that radically changed my life and laid the foundation for my jumping into the beloved life. As I rode toward the church, I heard music. Going behind the church to the parking lot, I saw a multiethnic crowd of what seemed like a thousand or so people standing and clapping. A multiethnic choir of close to a hundred people was leading the crowd. I simply stood in awe. It looked like heaven.

My very first connection with the church was as a child of about nine or ten years old. My aunt Robin would take me to a mostly white Lutheran church. From what I can remember, we were either the only African Americans there or part of just a handful. Whenever I would stay the weekend at my grandmother's house, Aunt Robin would take me to church with her. I believe we went to this church because it was within walking distance, being just a block away. Attending this church didn't last very long though. All I really remember was that the services were short and there were very few others who looked like us. About three years later I found myself at Redeemer Missionary Baptist Church, a predominantly African American congregation. This is the congregation where I really made the jump into connecting with a church. Through these two experiences, I had connected to the church in black and white. I really didn't know the church beyond these two pictures. I had experienced church as both the majority and the minority. It was as if no other church existed besides those two.

This is why my experience on the blacktop parking lot behind the Park Avenue United Methodist Church on that summer day was so powerful. I later learned that I was experiencing an evangelistic outreach called the Soul Liberation Festival. It was the vision of the youth pastor back then, Art Erickson. It was a weeklong urban revival of sorts, and I was hooked the moment I rode up on my bike. The gospel music drew me in, but I stayed because of the picture of the church that I saw. First, it was a church outside of a building's walls providing music, food, and a message of transformation in the city. Second, it was multiracial. To see African Americans, European Americans, Native Americans, and Latinos was just incredible to me! In my mind right then and there, I knew that was what church was supposed to look like.

I can remember as a kid having a couple of black-and-white television sets that had only five channels on them. We did have a color television as well, but we had just one, and it was the family television that to me felt like it was for special occasions. But it, too, had only five channels. To change the channel, you had to get up off the couch, walk to the television, and turn the knob with your hand. And if you reached back behind the television and flipped the UHF switch, you could get one more channel. A big antenna sat on top of the television to help the channels come in with more clarity if it was positioned just right.

I remember watching television shows in black and white. I also remember as things evolved in our house with the television. By the time I was in high school, we had multiple color television sets complete with cable. They all had remote controls so you no longer had to get up off the couch to turn the knob or deal with a UHF switch. Today I have all color televisions with digital cable. I have channels I don't even watch. I can't imagine having a black-and-white television in my house. And now, with networks going to all digital output, analog televisions have become nearly obsolete.

I bring up the television and its evolution from black and white with few channels to color, digital, and too many channels to watch to really portray what being at the Soul Liberation Festival did for me. I saw the church in full color for the first time! Before, I had seen the church in black and white, but I now saw a new picture of the church. I know that experiencing that event coupled with meeting Joey earlier that year was pivotal in my making the jump from just connecting with church to connecting deeply with God through Jesus Christ.

◆ ◆

After experiencing the Soul Liberation Festival that night, I came back during the rest of the week to experience more. There were black gospel choirs, white Christian rock bands, a Christian rap group, and even Southern gospel quartets. The speakers each night were awesome as well. One night I heard John Perkins, an African American from Mississippi who almost lost his life at the hands of whites who nearly beat him to death for fighting for equality during the early '70s. His response to that hatred was forgiveness, reconciliation, and love. I was so moved by his testimony that I bought his book *With Justice for All* that night and read about the three Rs: reconciliation, relocation, and redistribution. The next night I heard Tony Campolo talk about the challenge of Jesus upon the church to love the poor. The next night I heard Tom Skinner talk about how God desires to transform our lives and then use us to transform the city. As I'm writing this, I'm still so filled with the passion that was dispatched into my soul that week.

I came away from that event believing that the church is supposed to be multiethnic and a vehicle of compassion, justice, and mercy: a beloved church. I know that event planted the seeds for my planting an intentionally evangelical, multiethnic, urban church years later as an adult. My becoming a Christian was intimately connected to a new view of the church.

You see, once I experienced the church in color, I couldn't go back to the church in black and white. Now please hear me, I have much respect for the black church. I understand why the black church exists in the United States of America. It began as a forced church because African slaves were seen as less than human and there were questions as to whether they even had souls. African slaves were not allowed in some white churches or were relegated to the balcony or forced to stand outside looking through an open door hoping to hear the Word of God preached. Many times the only thing in those sermons directed toward the African slave was "Slaves, obey your masters." The black church began as a place that not only preached salvation but imparted humanness upon African slaves and later African Americans living in segregation. The black church has been an educational, financial, and leadership-development institute for a people finding solidarity in the biblical story of the exodus. Even today in many urban and predominantly rural African American communities, the black church is a place of social advocacy and spiritual empowerment. The black church was my first deep connection to the church as a place that provided a strong nurturing community for me outside of my family.

In no way do I desire to dishonor the black church. At the same time, the multiethnic picture of the church that I saw through the Soul Liberation Festival stirred something deep within me. How can Dr. Martin Luther King Jr.'s vision of the beloved community become more and more of a reality on earth? I began to be enveloped with the vision that a beloved church could dismantle racial segregation in the body of Christ. As a teenager, I became passionate to be a part of a post-black, post-white church. The words of John in the book of Revelation became the text that portrayed my passion:

> *After these things I looked, and behold, a great multitude which no one could count, from every nation and all tribes and peoples and tongues, standing before*

the throne and before the Lamb, clothed in white
robes, and palm branches were in their hands; and
they cry out with a loud voice, saying, "Salvation to
our God who sits on the throne, and to the Lamb."

Revelation 7:9–10

Those words from John, the disciple who gave so much of his writing in the Bible to dealing with the issue of belovedness, give this picture of the place where we will live eternally. I wanted on a regular basis to live in this type of liberated community. Yes, as I grew into an adult, I spent time back and forth between the white church and the black church, but I never lost my thirst for the beloved church.

The segregated church for me became like the walled-in area that contains the African impala at the zoo. There are walls that divide us by class, race, and culture. These barriers have led to a racially segregated worship experience in many churches on Sunday morning. In an ever-increasing multiethnic and multicultural world, this walled-in experience of corporate worship is not liberating, but limited. It keeps people from a Christ-centered experience that can serve as a sneak preview of heaven.

I believe the church must say yes to the journey of engaging this multicultural world and advancing the Kingdom of God within it.

This is about ourselves, one another, our churches, and ultimately our world. I know that sounds big, and you may be saying, "How in the world can I get involved in a movement that big?"

Don't miss this next sentence. God uses ordinary people to do extraordinary, Kingdom-building acts. That means people just like you and me, people living daily in the identity of the beloved self. And although one person can make a significant difference, a group of people such as a church can accomplish far more.

After I made the jump into an intimate relationship with God through Jesus Christ and then the jump into the post-black, post-white church, I began to have a greater sense of God's purpose for my life. I began to use my gifts to continue the vision of what I experienced the first time I came upon the Soul Liberation Festival. As I shared in chapter 2, I used my gift of singing to join a multiracial singing group called Brothers in Christ. By my freshman year in college, I was in a new singing group called Soul Purpose. This group featured me, a young African American woman named Yolanda, and a young European American woman named Lana. I was from Minneapolis, Yolanda from Chicago, and Lana from a small town in Michigan called Hillsdale. Yolanda had a fabulous black gospel sound that caused people to clap and shout when she sang. Lana brought both a Southern gospel and contemporary Christian sound. My job was to flow between, sort of a Larnelle Harris and Fred Hammond sound in order to provide an urban gospel and contemporary Christian flavor. We started by singing at the Soul Liberation Festival the summer after my senior year in high school. From there we sang at urban, suburban, and rural church events all over the country.

We were using our gifts, and we were also providing a picture of the beloved church.

This is where the jump into being used by God to build the beloved church begins: Start with the gifts God has given you to advance His Kingdom on earth. The Bible is full of stories of God using people—men and women, boys and girls—to advance His Kingdom. God used David to take on a giant. God used Josiah at eight years old to become king in order to bring God's ordinances and statutes back to the center and foundation of a nation. God used a girl named Esther by making her queen and keeping her people from death. God used Nehemiah to rebuild a city. The stories go on and on throughout the Scriptures. The question is not *will* God use us but *how* will God use us.

◆ ◆

Dwight Robertson, president of Kingdom Building Ministries in Denver, Colorado, expresses this liberating life of being used by God in his book *You Are God's Plan A (And There Is No Plan B)*. We are God's plan for changing the world; that's the way it has always been. We can be a vehicle of God, a laborer of the Kingdom, simply by utilizing our gifts to show the world a more biblical church, a beloved church. By singing in Soul Purpose, I was using the specific gift that God had placed in me. And by singing with Lana and Yolanda, I was using my gifts in community to do something that I would not have been able to do alone. The fact that our group was diverse and multiethnic also provided us the opportunity to go into churches that were divided by denomination and race in order to give a picture of the beloved church. During that time I learned so much about what happens when we make the jump of allowing God to use us to give a picture of what the church should really look like. What is just as important is that by being used by God in this way, I learned more about what my life should really look like—a life that gives God glory through using the gifts He gave me for His purposes. God was showing me how my passion intersects with my purpose. The experience of the Soul Liberation Festival helped crystallize a passion that had been in me for a long time. Seeing the diversity of that evangelistic and outreach event was pivotal in my later understanding of my passion for issues such as reconciliation and the church as a Christ-centered and multiethnic community.

Both of my parents are from the South. My mother is from Birmingham, Alabama, and my father is from Monroe, Louisiana. They both understand segregation at its worst. They know colored-only water fountains and bathrooms. They know not being able to go to school with white students. They know sitting in the back of the bus.

On the other hand, I was born in 1969, a member of the post–civil rights generation, and I grew up in the integrated Midwest, specifically in Minnesota. You really can't get much farther north in the United States of America than where I lived. It's not that issues of racism and prejudice no longer exist, but I've grown up in a reality that allows me to dream dreams and long for something far beyond what my parents experienced growing up in the segregated South. The church divided by black and white made sense to my parents' generation based on their cultural context. But thank God, Dr. Martin Luther King Jr. cast a vision for something different. Through his moving sermons and insightful and theologically challenging writings he presented a framework for what he called the beloved community. I see this framework as a mainstream and nationwide articulation of the Kingdom of God showing up in the earth for purposes of transformation both spiritually and socially. Because of this Christ-centered, church-based movement, I was able to grow up in a radically different society than my parents did.

Yes, there is still a need for more change, especially Kingdom change, in our society, but I'm blessed to be on the other side of the transformation that came from the vision and strategy for a beloved community.

I've never had to drink from a colored-only water fountain. I've never been forced to sit in the back of the bus. Every school I've attended has been multiethnic, some more than others (Saint John's being the near exception). Growing up in this kind of reality caused me to question a church for the most part still divided by race. It was weird to me to go to school all week and experience racial diversity, but then on Sunday be faced with the option of having to choose between black or white. This didn't seem right to me. The whole world outside of the church seemed to be in full color, but the church looked like the black-and-white television of the old days. As James 3:10 says, "My brothers, this should not be" (NIV).

The multiethnic world I lived in made the church look just plain odd to me. I understood from stories from my parents and grandparents why the church was divided by race, but it just didn't make sense to me. I dreamed of a different church, and even a different world, far from the one that my parents grew up in.

With each jump further into God, I felt more and more freedom. God was giving me clarity around my purpose through my passion for a multiethnic church and also through the gifts He placed in me. Jeremiah 1 gives the biblical foundation for this:

> *Before I formed you in the womb I knew you, and before you were born I consecrated you.*
>
> **Jeremiah 1:5**

◆ ◆

Before I was even born into this world, God placed gifts in me that connect with my passion and clarify my purpose in Him. I have had a love for music and theater for as long as I can remember. I've always enjoyed getting up in front of people and singing or acting. I was the one at family gatherings who would be called upon to sing or do something funny in front of people, and I was very comfortable with that. As I grew up, I was constantly involved in school plays and choir. Drama and music were the gifts that God had placed in me and pointed to the unique way in which I was formed and consecrated.

Now I need to mention here that I don't want to take this point too far. Our gifts are important, but they are not the foundation of our identity. Our identity is in Christ. Our identity is in the beloved self, one who is well loved by God through Jesus Christ.

> *Now when all the people were baptized, Jesus was also baptized, and while He was praying, heaven was opened, and the Holy Spirit descended upon Him in bodily form like a dove, and a voice came out of heaven, "You are My beloved Son, in You I am well-pleased."*
>
> **Luke 3:21–22**

I'll never forget a conversation I had with my mother when I told her that I had become a Christian and that I wanted to use my gift of singing and drama for Christ. She told me that when she was pregnant with me, she had a dream that my grandmother came to her and said, "The baby that is in your womb will do great things for God." I must admit this decree moved me, but as a teenager it scared me to death! I told my mother that I was also having dreams of being up on a stage in front of a large and diverse group of people, but I didn't know exactly what I was doing in the dream. She told me that over time God would show me. "Maybe you're to be a preacher," she said. At the time, I didn't want to hear that! That would be another jump for another day. But I began to connect my gifts with my passion, and even though I was only a teenager, I was able to experience being used by God to advance His Kingdom. I sang in music groups and used my acting gifts with a Christian theater company called Actors for Christ.

The next summer I attended a family reunion on my mother's side. One evening one of my cousins, who is a genealogist, gave a presentation on our family tree. She stated that my great-great-grandfather was full-blooded Irish and that he married a woman who was Cherokee Indian and African American. Through this African American and Indian woman, we could also trace my family tree back to a slave woman named Easter. Even though she was a slave, she had a name that pointed to our opportunity to jump into the beloved life, made possible through the resurrection of Jesus. They had a son, my great-grandfather, who was so light skinned that he could pass for white. As I listened to her tell the story of my family tree, the fact that my grandfather had shiny, long, straight hair and was also very light skinned made more sense. My mother is light skinned as well. So are my two daughters. I left that family reunion realizing that not only am I ethnically African American but I'm also Irish and Cherokee Indian. I am a multiethnic human being!

This reality also explains my deep passion for a beloved church that is not divided by race. This news was fresh to me, but not to God. God knew in advance that my passion, gifts, family tree, and personal relationship with Him through Jesus would all combine to call me to jump into my Kingdom purpose. Each of these ingredients was needed to shape my call to work with others to develop the beloved church. You see, when I started out, I felt I was just a black kid. But over time, I began to see that I was much more than the world thought I was. In fact, I was much more than my family members or even my pastor could see. This knowledge grew by jumping a number of times deeper into God's love. By living in the beloved self, I began to see myself more and more as God sees me, and He sees me through the lens of His Son, the beloved One in whom He is well pleased. My identity in Christ and the gifts placed in me by the Father and activated through the Holy Spirit qualify me to build the beloved church.

Are you willing to wrestle with how God wants to use you to advance His Kingdom? How can you play a role in building the beloved church? Remember, it starts by jumping into God's great love for you and then jumping into God's great Kingdom purpose for your life.

Chapter 5

RECONCILIATION

And He had to pass through Samaria.

John 4:4

As beloved children of God, we all can play a role on some level in building the beloved church. When Dr. Martin Luther King Jr. spoke of the beloved community, he was speaking of a reality in which racial division was dismantled. The church ought to be the community that models to the broader society the fullness of the reconciling work completed by Jesus on the cross.

In the United States, Sunday morning at eleven o'clock is unfortunately still the most segregated hour of the week. In our ever-increasing multiethnic and multicultural world, this is why we desperately need sisters and brothers who will say *yes* to the development of a reconciling church. Jesus is the chief reconciler. Reconciliation is made possible only through Him.

There was cultural and ethnic division in Jesus' day, and yet He chose to be a bridge across that divide. The Jewish and Samaritan divide was one that Jesus stepped into for the sake of Kingdom advancement, and we would do well to follow His lead. Jesus decided to jump right into the center of the Jewish and Samaritan divide. This experience of social division can be compared to the historic black and white divide in the United States. Today though, the diversity of our nation is so much bigger than black and white that we can't afford to let this historic divide limit the possibilities of the Kingdom community that can be realized. I believe the experience of Jesus with the Samaritan woman at the well is a strategic blueprint for advancing the beloved church.

John 4:4 says that Jesus had to go to Samaria. This verse points more to a Kingdom mandate from the Father than a geographical necessity. He could have found a way in His travel plans to avoid Samaria altogether, but His Kingdom mission would not allow it. Likewise, we could avoid building the beloved church, a church that dismantles the racial divide. We could continue to maintain and plant churches that are homogeneous, but there is a Kingdom mandate upon us as well. We could give in to a social default button, which leads us to worship in comfort with people who are like us, or we can choose the uncomfortable Kingdom mandate that compels us to create a more Christ-centered and reconciling community. If we are truly in an intimate relationship with God through Jesus Christ, it should be that we cannot help but become reconcilers. I say this because racial divisions do not restrict God's love, and this type of love resides in us, His beloved children. We are reconciled to God through Jesus Christ, and simultaneously we are empowered to become reconcilers in the world. In Jesus is the healing necessary to deal with any social division we face. The chief reconciler makes an army of reconcilers possible. Paul lays this out in 2 Corinthians 5.

Now all these things are from God, who reconciled us to Himself through Christ and gave us the ministry of reconciliation, namely, that God was in Christ reconciling the world to Himself, not counting their trespasses against them, and He has committed to us the word of reconciliation. Therefore, we are ambassadors for Christ, as though God were making an appeal through us; we beg you on behalf of Christ, be reconciled to God.

2 Corinthians 5:18–20

Did you catch that? God, through Paul, begs the church at Corinth to be reconciled. The church at Corinth was a diverse, multicultural community. This congregation and its struggles show us the need for the progression that I've been laying out. It begins with the beloved self, moves to the beloved church, and then to the beloved world. Without this progression, credibility issues arise in advancing the Kingdom. The force of being reconciled to God ought to be so great that we can't contain it. It leads us to become reconcilers in the world ourselves. Christ makes reconciliation possible and then through the Holy Spirit passes on the mission of reconciliation to us until He returns. The life of Jesus on earth serves as a strategy of how to live the life of an ambassador of reconciliation. We are representatives of the Kingdom and the King of reconciliation.

This part of the beloved life begins with being willing to go *there,* to that place of reconciliation. The well where Jesus meets the Samaritan woman is a place of reconciliation. But how do we do it? How do we enter these "well" places?

◆ ◆

This was the question I set out to answer corporately when I said yes to planting a church that would be intentionally evangelical, multi-ethnic, and urban. In 2003, I made this jump into church planting in Minneapolis. I now had the opportunity to develop and lead the kind of church that I had envisioned since I became a Christian. John 4 served as a biblical strategy for the birthing of the Sanctuary Covenant Church. Jesus going to Samaria and the story that unfolded there needed to become on some level the story of a core team with a vision to develop the beloved church. And while this was a corporate journey on one level, I also realized the need to revisit my individual life in terms of where I was as a reconciler.

For Jesus it was not just going to Samaria but putting Himself in the position to receive from a Samaritan woman. As the woman came to the well for water, Jesus requested a drink. Here is Jesus, the Son of God, asking a Samaritan woman, a second-class citizen to the

Jewish male that He was, for a drink. In spite of the social construct, which provided their class and gender separation, He became the reconciler. By asking her for a drink, He opened the way for a deeper conversation.

Many of us experience the reality of living in a diverse society on a daily basis, but do we purposely put ourselves in a position to have a need met by someone of another ethnicity? Do we experience serving and being served cross-culturally? Maybe it begins with being willing to engage in conversation cross-culturally. For some of us, this means being willing to jump over whatever social wall is keeping us from this Kingdom call.

This is where my wife and I began in the planting of the Sanctuary Covenant Church. We met in homes and began conversations with people across race. The mainstream social structures of church would say that this was not the way to plant a church, but like Jesus had to go to Samaria, we had to go there in our context. I say this because I've attended workshops and forums on church planting where the advice was given to plant in a more homogeneous way. But what if you have a burden for something else? What about the multiethnic and multicultural reality all around us? I wrestled with these types of questions as we set out to plant a beloved church.

In the development of a core team for this multiethnic church, we moved from meeting in homes to meeting in the basement of an existing church within our same denomination. These gatherings included potluck meals, singing a few worship songs together, and then my leading a Bible study and sharing the vision for this new church. For the potluck meals, we asked people to bring dishes representing their culture and upbringing. We had lasagna next to the fried rice, and collard greens next to the green bean casserole. The thought was that we digest one another's food to set up building the kind of reconciling relationships that can digest one another's stories. To start this process, we would also go around the room and share stories about ourselves. I was amazed at the diversity and depth of experiences in that place. There is something powerful about being intentional about Christ-centered, multiethnic community. And like Jesus, you need only be willing to go there.

Our core team meetings for our church plant became reconciling environments. However, you don't have to embark on a church plant to do this. Your home can become a reconciling community just by taking advantage of the diversity in your neighborhood or at your place of work. A few years ago my wife took on a job at the public high school where we both graduated. She worked in the career and counseling center along with a European American woman named Nora. She could have limited her relationship with Nora to just a working one, but not my wife. As long as I've known her, she has always been willing to go there, to develop beloved relationships across ethnicity and race. I learn a lot from watching her. She takes advantage of the opportunities to build reconciling relationships, and soon a coworker is an extended family member. Nora worked with my wife, but she also attended high school basketball games with our family and on a number of occasions sat with us at our kitchen counter. This is how it should be, about the expansion of God's family in a diverse world. To do this, we must be willing to explore the three-foot walls that keep us from taking the jump into reconciliation. Is it fear? Is it prejudice? Is it that someone of a different ethnicity who mistreated us in the past? What is keeping you from taking the jump?

Not everyone takes heed to this beloved call. There were others who were Jewish like Jesus who weren't willing to go there and sit at the well with a Samaritan woman. But Jesus had a Kingdom mission to advance the beloved world. When I think of my wife, Donecia, that's what I see: a woman on a reconciling mission. It's not an easy jump, but most things worth doing aren't easy.

◆ ◆

I want to go back to the African impala story that I began this book with for a moment. Remember, one of the reasons that the African impala can be contained by a three-foot wall is because if it can't see where it's going to land, it won't jump. Some of us are hesitant to build multiethnic and reconciling communities because we don't know where we will land. What if tension arises? What if I say something offensive? What if I'm misunderstood? What if it turns out like the last time, when I took this jump and it didn't go well? Jumping into the journey of reconciling community is, as Forrest Gump would say, "like a box of chocolates. You never know what you're gonna get."

We must be willing to go beyond surface relationships cross-culturally to a deeper, more intimate, Christ-centered journey with one another. This is not easy, but it is possible. I know I've struggled with staying committed when confronted with the cost of reconciliation. As an African American, I want to pull away when I'm offended by a European American, but I must hang in there. I've failed in cross-cultural relationships on many levels. The honest truth is relationships with people "like us" are just easier. We are conditioned in our society to find comfort and safety in homogeneous communities. But Kingdom community looks different than homogeneous community.

I encountered this struggle as a teenager. I had a number of African American friends in my neighborhood—Tony, Kevin, Steve, and Mike. I also remember a European American kid named John who lived at the end of my block. I liked John. We rode bikes together and played basketball and soccer together. I acted as if we were closer friends when it was just the two of us, but when my African American friends came around, I treated John differently. I was not willing to fully jump into our cross-cultural friendship. Soon our friendship grew apart, and he and his family moved away from the neighborhood.

Years later as an adult, I developed a strong friendship with a European American brother named Paul. I say brother because we were both Christians and worked full-time in ministry. We met because we both worked for sports ministries. We also lived in the same community. We would meet once a week in the morning, jog around a lake for exercise, and pray together. At the time, I was also serving as a volunteer youth minister at an African American church. It feels bad to admit this, but I separated my relationship with Paul from my life in the African American church community. Soon Paul moved to Michigan, and a little over a year later I moved with my family to Ohio. Paul continued to try to stay close by reaching out to me, but I didn't do a great job of reaching back to him. I had a chance to journey deeper in a reconciling relationship, but I just wasn't willing to make the jump.

Even more recently, I've witnessed that I can still struggle in living out reconciling relationships. I preached an Easter sermon last year in which I talked about the need to be connected to the authentic Jesus instead of being involved with a connection that divides us by race. What I meant by that was lifting up a biblical Jesus instead of a white Jesus or a black Jesus. Using John 15 as my text and "Abiding in the Vine" as my title, I raised the question: "Which vine are you connected to?" I talked about a church in the United States that seems to be clinging to multiple versions of Jesus. Some are abiding in the black Jesus and others the white Jesus. The big idea of the sermon was that if we are truly going to be a reconciling church, we are going to have to abide in the biblical Jesus, a multiethnic and multicultural Jesus who is both the Son of God and the Son of Man. With passion, sweat, and tears I preached about the biblical Jesus who is also relevant in an ever-increasing multiethnic and multicultural society. I spoke clearly about racism as a demonic force as well.

The next morning a man in our congregation, who happens to be European American, called the office and expressed his deep concern with parts of my sermon. Even though we talked by phone and in person days later, I carried this around in my heart for a long time. Not only was I bothered because he didn't approve of a sermon focused on issues I'm very passionate about, but also, because he happens to be a European American male, I was struggling with race issues that I realized still needed to be dealt with in my own life. Thank God we both took the jump to deepen our relationship and are living in the journey of the beloved church. Is there an opportunity to go deeper in a reconciling relationship staring you in the face that you are not taking advantage of? Are you ignoring this opportunity to build the beloved church?

◆ ◆

It could be that we're ignoring this because it's just plain hard. We don't have the power in and of ourselves to sustain beloved and reconciling relationships. We must be empowered by God daily to build the beloved church. This is why reconciliation cannot be seen as simply a social behavior but rather a spiritual discipline. Reconciliation must be seen as a vital component of our Christian formation. Some evangelicals shun the attention the beloved church should have in their lives because they see reconciliation as merely a social act of political correctness. Reconciliation is not liberal political ideology but Kingdom-building work! Our maturity as Christians ought to be measured in part by our ability to live in reconciling community. This is not an easy journey though. I've struggled in this journey of Christian formation and spiritual maturity. But even with this reality, God's grace has kept me on the road of reconciliation. The One who completes the work of reconciliation empowers me to keep trying and keep going. I believe these struggles played a role in God's leading me into church planting and have kept me in a multiethnic and reconciling church even when things are hard.

When Donecia and I started out on the journey of planting an intentionally multiethnic, Christ-centered, and reconciling community, we weren't sure what we were going to get or where we were going to land. What we were sure of was our desire to be a part of a church that could advance God's Kingdom in a multicultural world. We wanted to be a part of a church that looked like heaven.

What I like about Jesus asking the Samaritan woman for a drink is that He was giving up something: namely, His privilege over her. Jesus set aside how culture defined Him and sat at a level of equality with her. This is so needed in the beloved church—setting aside our worldly labels and categories in order to have a more biblically authentic relationship with one another. Let me be very clear: The racial construct of black and white is unbiblical. This categorizing and placing value on someone based on skin color is ungodly. The race structure cannot be justified as we move through and wrestle with Scripture. Culture, ethnicity, and nationality are biblical, but not race. But even these characteristics are trumped by our identity through Christ in the beloved self. Our differences then become primarily a platform to celebrate the great creativity of our God. In developing reconciling community we must look at what we are willing to give up to build community at the well. At the same time we must honor our cultural and ethnic diversity. When we do this first and foremost as recognizing the creative genius of our God, this becomes an act of worship.

In order to develop our Christ-centered, multiethnic community known as the Sanctuary Covenant Church, we needed people who were willing to give up the comfort of the all-black church, the all-white church, or the all-Asian church. By having potluck meals in our core team development, people had to give up eating only foods they were accustomed to. And sitting at the table together, or the well together, opened up the opportunity for dialogue.

> *Therefore the Samaritan woman said to Him, "How is it that You, being a Jew, ask me for a drink since I am a Samaritan woman?" (For Jews have no dealings with Samaritans.)*
>
> **John 4:9**

The Samaritan woman speaks to the reality of the Jews and the Samaritans being separated. We must be willing to acknowledge that the church's picture is in black and white. The church remains disconnected from its broader Kingdom mission in the world by being segregated by an unbiblical social construct. The building of the beloved church will raise questions. I still remember when our church began weekly worship experiences. When we first began, we were about 70 percent European American. Some asked, "Why are all those white people coming?" This question to me is asked in the same manner as the Samaritan woman questioning why Jesus would ask her for a drink. This reminds me of another moment when I realized the reconciling commitment of my wife.

I recall the Sunday we had our Grand Opening Worship Experience of the Sanctuary Covenant Church. As the worship experience was about to start, I felt like a little kid in his first school play. I looked out behind a curtain on the stage of the high school auditorium where we were meeting. I kept seeing so many white people coming in. It was as if my wife knew what I was thinking. She said, "What are you going to do if all these white people come back next week?" Before I could answer she said, "You're going to pastor them."

The notion of an African American leading a predominantly European American church may be a strange sight to many. Isn't a black pastor supposed to lead a black congregation? Don't black people go to black church and white people go to white church? You see, whether the question is about the Samaritan woman or my leading a predominantly European American church plant, the problem exposed is the same. The reality of the social construct is blinding the biblical mandate. The authority and centrality of Scripture, which are evangelical enduring values, should alone lead us to dismantle the segregated church in the United States.

Jesus answered and said to her, "If you knew the gift of God, and who it is who says to you, 'Give Me a drink,' you would have asked Him, and He would have given you living water."

John 4:10

Jesus tells the Samaritan woman about a gift. This gift is embodied in Jesus Himself. He is living water. He is reconciliation completed. He is the gift to be experienced in the beloved church.

We get the opportunity to experience reconciliation as well as the reconciler in a deeper way in the Christ-centered and multiethnic community. I experience something beyond what words can truly explain when I'm in a multiethnic worship experience. Let me take you to one of the Sunday-morning experiences of worship while I was pastor at the Sanctuary Covenant Church.

◆ ◆

It's the beginning of the spring season in Minnesota (which means there could still be a chance for a blizzard at any time), and on this particular Sunday morning an experience of corporate worship is about to begin that is a continuation of the last seven weeks on racial reconciliation. These worship experiences are tied to a broader campaign of the church known as Vision for the City. For the entire year there will be a focus on the purpose of the church: to change the face of the church by reconciling the people of the city to God and one another as well as stewardship. The hope is that by focusing on reconciliation and stewardship, we would own the core values, purpose, and vision of the church collectively as a community. The Vision for the City campaign includes not only what goes on through the experience of corporate worship on Sunday morning but also an all-church Bible study on racial reconciliation and multiethnic in-home fellowship gatherings during the week. The hope is this will play a role in the increase of multiethnic community groups within the church.

The praise and worship begins with our experience of corporate worship director Sherrie Jones giving an opening prayer and then leading a time of praise and worship that includes the sounds of hip-hop, soul, rock licks, and urban gospel. Our praise and worship band on any given Sunday can go from sounding like Earth, Wind & Fire to Kirk Franklin to the David Crowder Band. We have a multiethnic group of singers and hip-hop emcees, enabling us to worship God through song in various styles to reach our multiethnic congregation and surrounding community. Though we have the ability to worship in a variety of ways through song, the sound most often heard is very soulful and urban.

One might ask why we do this instead of presenting a mix of genres and styles to reach a multiethnic congregation. The African American urban music sound has been a universal sound that has brought people of many cultures and ethnicities together in America. Jazz, the Motown sound, and now hip-hop have been able to influence and build bridges across race in a way that other music styles have not. Mix this reality with something more important, which is a desire to lead a multiethnic congregation in a corporate experience of worship, and now you have something pretty powerful on your hands! At the time of this particular worship experience Sanctuary was more balanced ethnically. Still, 55 percent of our congregation is European American, and yet most Sundays our praise and worship style is hip-hop, neo soul, and urban gospel. In many ways this is just proving my point about the influence of African American and urban music to actually emerge into the music of America and the music of the world.

Through this style of praise and worship, we were able to grow in just over four years into an intergenerational and multiethnic community of one thousand, with a membership of close to four hundred. I mention intergenerational because the children do not depart to our Royal Hood Children's ministry until after our time of praise and worship. Also, it should be mentioned, because of our contemporary and relevant approach to the experience of corporate worship, youth stay in the experience the whole time. I'm not saying this to suggest that everyone is at Sanctuary because of the praise and worship style. There have been some who have admitted to me that the music is not really their personal taste, but to be in an atmosphere that models a sneak preview of heaven on earth makes it hard for them not to be drawn in and even move to something beyond just a tolerance of Sanctuary's praise and worship style. There is a Spirit-led, organic "something" that takes place at the Sanctuary Covenant Church that is very difficult to put words to, but I believe if we are willing to live in this "something," it will lead on a larger scale to the future of the church in the United States and beyond.

After the praise and worship, we have a "meet and greet" time, which I believe is important when it comes to attempting each week to move from being an ethnically and racially diverse crowd to a multiethnic and reconciling community. Before the sermon, members of our Reconciliation Design Team present a dramatic, spoken-word piece entitled "Where I'm From." The piece is presented by a multiethnic group of women and men who tell the unique ethnic stories of their upbringing, faith story, and personal take on the world around them. They end the piece by asking in unison, "Where are you from?" The point here is to proclaim that though we desire to live in a Christ-centered and reconciling community, we can still celebrate our biblically based diversity. By biblically based, I mean we celebrate ethnicity, culture, and language, but not race.

After the spoken-word piece, I preach a sermon entitled "Reconciliation and Worship," which ends with an altar call with people of all different backgrounds committing to and praying through becoming ambassadors of reconciliation. As I look at the people praying in front of the stage in the auditorium at Patrick Henry High School in Minneapolis, I am overtaken by the picture before me. I'm awed, speechless, frozen, warm, and for a moment even removed from the fact that I'm the senior pastor of this church. I look up at the larger group of multiethnic people and I say to myself, "How did this happen?" and also, "Thank You, Lord, for the opportunity to be a part of this!" I'm experiencing the gift of sitting at the well and drinking the living water of reconciliation.

I realize in that moment that this is something special and out of the norm for the church in America. The Sanctuary Covenant Church is not the only multiethnic church in the United States, but it doesn't represent the majority of churches in America either. This is why I call Sanctuary a post-black, post-white church. It is abnormal in a society that has accepted homogeneous and segregated church as normal church. Church normalcy today is like how the Samaritan woman put it when she said that Jews and Samaritans have no dealings with each other. However, the beloved church is one that is willing to go against the cultural norms of the society around it, to give that society a picture of what can be. But it takes more than just sitting together as a multiethnic assembly on Sunday morning to experience the beloved church.

On another occasion minister, author, and Bethel University

reconciliation studies professor Dr. Curtiss DeYoung preached a sermon at our church in which he said something I have yet to forget. As he looked at our multiethnic congregation, he said, "You have become a truly multicultural congregation, but you have yet to become a reconciling community." At first, I wondered what he was saying. Were we doing something wrong? What were we not doing right? I learned later that he meant that it would take more than a Sunday-morning experience of worship to become a beloved church. We would have to work to develop other ministry initiatives to cause us to deal with the issues that tend to keep us divided. We have to be willing to, as one of our original core team members said, "get messy." Though Jesus offered the Samaritan woman a gift, He also raised the messy issue that needed to be dealt with, the elephant at the well, if you will.

He said to her, "Go, call your husband and come here." The woman answered and said, "I have no husband." Jesus said to her, "You have correctly said, 'I have no husband'; for you have had five husbands, and the one whom you now have is not your husband; this you have said truly."

John 4:16–18

Jesus brought up the issue of a sinful life. He raised the issue that she maybe wasn't interested in dealing with that day. If we are truly going to build the beloved church, we must be willing to raise uncomfortable issues. We put on initiatives such as all-church Bible studies on reconciliation. We had an all-day forum on authentic dialogue across culture and race. Through our denomination we had a two-day initiative entitled The Invitation to Racial Righteousness. We talked about the hard issue of privilege and marginalization. We talked about the history of slavery and Jim Crow segregation in our country. We talked about racial stereotypes and prejudice that keep us from being unified the way God would desire us to be. There were moments during these initiatives when things got tense, but we had to be willing to get messy. Teaching Pastor Helen Musick of Quest Community Church in Lexington, Kentucky, once said that in order for there to be reconciliation within a community, there must be disequilibration first. This means a storm, a bit of chaos within the community. But if this is a Christ-centered community, we must remember that Jesus is neither startled nor surprised by the storms that arise on the journey of reconciliation. Jesus is the One who calms the storms.

> *The woman said to Him, "Sir, I perceive that You are a prophet. Our fathers worshiped in this mountain, and you people say that in Jerusalem is the place where men ought to worship." Jesus said to her, "Woman, believe Me, an hour is coming when neither in this mountain nor in Jerusalem will you worship the Father.... But an hour is coming, and now is, when the true worshipers will worship the Father in spirit and truth; for such people the Father seeks to be His worshipers."*

John 4:19–21, 23

◆ ◆

This kind of worship is a lifestyle. The beloved life is a reconciling life, and reconciliation doesn't take place fully in a corporate experience of worship on Sunday morning alone. Yes, we must be willing to worship together corporately in a way that dismantles walls of ethnic and racial division, but we must also be willing to build authentic, reconciling relationships with one another. This has led our church to develop ministries and facilitate experiences that further develop cross-cultural community. The church facilitating organic cross-cultural community experiences is vital. As churches grow, they can become more and more program focused. Ministry programs, which could include classes, mission experiences, and retreats, aren't bad and can be great opportunities for spiritual growth and Kingdom advancement. But what we also need in the beloved church are just more opportunities to hang out with one another in order to develop more authentic relationships. Think of the times when Jesus was simply hanging out with people. We find Jesus on many occasions simply sitting at a table having a meal, hanging out in the crowd, or on a boat with His disciples. In this diverse and busy world we live in today, it's easy to lose sight of the significance of hanging out with one another. We must think through how to create environments where people can keep it real and build trust, so a more multiethnic community can truly be a reality. Maybe your church is at a place where you don't need another class or program; you just simply need one another.

Most of our ministry models are not unique, but the fact that they're being developed and worked out in an intentionally multi-ethnic and reconciling community is what makes them special. There is something powerful about worshipping together, praying for one another, walking with each other in our spiritual growth, and meeting each other's needs cross-culturally. This is the journey of the beloved church.

Chapter 6

ENGAGE

I do not ask You to take them out of the world, but to keep them from the evil one.

John 17:15

The beloved church is one that understands that it must engage culture for Kingdom purposes. Coming to terms on how to live as God's beloved in the culture around us is crucial. The culture here is being defined as the emerging, developing world. It's what's around us—both good and bad, divine and demonic, wonderful and dangerous. Within all of that are values, language, fashion, art, and a bunch of subcultures. All of this can be very complex, but also a tremendous opportunity for the church to offer God's love to the world. In a general sense the church has taken two approaches in its relationship with culture. One is to see culture as the enemy, and the other is to embrace the culture.

In seeing the culture as the enemy, we take a position of being primarily at war. I firmly believe this hinders the church's ability to be a force of love within culture. Over the years I've witnessed a couple of ways in which seeing the culture as the enemy plays out. One is by defining the culture as the world of those living in the old life, the life of sin. The culture is then the dwelling place for sinners. At the core of this position is "Before I became a Christian, I was in the world, but now that I'm a believer, I'm in the world no longer." As a teenager, when I would hear Christians say, "I'm no longer in the world," I wanted to blurt out, "Well, what planet do you live on now?" It stands, then, that the church is a place of refuge from the culture, a safe, Spirit-filled escape from the world.

When I was growing up, I had many friends in churches that took this position on culture. My friends attended churches that had developed a list of all the places you shouldn't go and all the things you shouldn't do in order to not be involved in the things of this world. In place of spending time in the world, they spent a lot of time in the church. The strategy of these types of churches was to keep you in the church building and participating in church activities as much as possible so that you wouldn't be corrupted by the world. Many times I felt guilty about some of the places I was going and things I was participating in when I was around them. At the same time I really wasn't interested in being in a church building every day of the week. I still feel this way today. However, I agree that there are places and activities that Christians should think critically about, no question.

I believe in the necessity of the new birth, so some of what my friends were proclaiming made sense to me. When we jump into the love of God and are transformed through Jesus Christ and the indwelling of the Holy Spirit, we ought to look carefully at our lives. The key is that we do this based on a healthy interpretation of the Scriptures. With this in mind, it made sense to me in making the jump into the beloved life to understand clearly the Bible's stance on issues such as drunkenness, lying, selfishness, and sex outside of marriage. But I struggled with my friends who saw going to school dances, listening to all forms of secular music, and playing cards as sinful. This is a legalism based on issues the Bible doesn't speak clearly on.

I remember being influenced at times by these Christian friends of mine. On one occasion, I threw away all of my secular music. This included rhythm and blues such as Stevie Wonder and Earth, Wind & Fire, as well as hip-hop artists like Run-DMC and Grandmaster Flash and the Furious Five. I regret doing that to this day. I could have at least taken them to the used-record store and gotten some money back for them, but I just threw them in the trash because I was trying not to live in the world any longer. I really didn't feel any love by being around these types of Christians, but I did feel a lot of guilt. I went through a back-and-forth existence at this point in my Christian life based on the types of Christians I was hanging out with.

During this time in my Christian life, my only reason for hanging out with non-Christians was for the purpose of leading them to Christ. Evangelism is a biblical mandate, but so is being an extension of God's love. In the Bible we read about Jesus healing the sick, casting demons out of people, and advocating for a woman who was about to receive the death penalty. What we don't know in every case is whether that person followed the teachings of Jesus and advanced the Kingdom from that point forward. In some cases, such as the Samaritan woman Jesus met at the well, we do see a more holistic transformation that takes place. She goes away from this experience to expand the Kingdom among her people (John 4). The common denominator in all of these encounters with Jesus is that they experienced the compassion and love of God. Christians who see culture as the enemy lose out on these opportunities to love as God loves.

When I hung out exclusively with Christians, we became almost a sort of Christian gang. We didn't wear the same colors or commit criminal activity, but we definitely had an attitude. To many we seemed arrogant and judgmental. We saw unchurched non-Christians merely as a part of an evangelism model, which was rehearsed and not relational or loving. This model operated on the basis of guilt; if you didn't accept our proposition in the end, you felt guilty. Our proposition was not just about receiving Jesus Christ as Lord and Savior but also about removing oneself from the ways of the world with a mix of issues, some clearly defined by the Bible and others that were not.

Now the irony of this was that many of my Christian friends who took this position toward the culture struggled just as much if not more than the people out there in the culture. Being in church all the time and not listening to secular music didn't automatically lead them to living any better than those who had yet to make a decision to follow Jesus. This is because living the Christian life is about a love relationship, not a law mandate. It takes a love identity in Christ in order to live as God desires us to. This is what living in the beloved self is about. There are many Christians who have the wrong perspective on culture because they have the wrong perspective on who God is and who they are in God. If we see God as One who loves us only based on what we do or where we go (more like what we don't do and where we don't go), then we easily look down on the culture around us and those living in it.

This staying out of the world to earn God's love and favor is a hard life to live, not to mention unbiblical. God loved us when we were *in the world,* and He loves us now, no more and no less. God loves us so much that through Jesus Christ we can receive life transformation and the opportunity to live in intimacy as God's beloved on a daily basis. Those living in the law have a hard time relating to the culture God's way because they have the wrong perspective on themselves. This spiritual identity disorder causes them to withhold God's love from others. I can remember a lot of my friends who lived this way, not the best people to hang around. They just weren't very loving. Imagine that—Christians not being loving. If you're not loving, how can you be living as God's beloved? To be the beloved is to be loved and loving at the same time. God's love within us cannot be contained. I had friends who had God's law in them, but not God's love. This was not entirely their fault; they were only teenagers. It was mainly because law-filled pastors and other adults in the church were beating this into them. They were not free. In some cases they were just as bound as those who didn't know Jesus as Savior. If you are law-filled instead of love-filled, you are not experiencing the freedom of the beloved life.

This all became very hard for me because I began to separate myself from many of my "old" friends, friends I had before I became a Christian. I stopped hanging out with people who didn't go to church or listened to secular music. Now, I understand that if you became a Christian and you previously hung out with a very bad crowd, separation could be a very wise choice for your Christian growth. That's not what I'm talking about. What I am talking about is someone who jumps into the love of God but refuses to jump into being empowered by God to love those who have yet to jump into God's love themselves. By making culture the enemy, we make those who are in the culture enemies. Unfortunately, I have been one of these law-filled Christians at times in my life. I talked to non-Christians as if I was better than them. I looked down upon them and judged them, not realizing how non-Christian I was behaving. Even today, I sometimes go to concerts or pass by events and see Christians protesting. In many cases they are right on the issues but wrong in the heart. The question becomes: Are God's children primarily to be an extension of His judgment or His love? I believe emphatically that it is the latter.

◆ ◆

This leads me to the second way of seeing culture as the enemy. In this position God is primarily, if not exclusively, in the church, and Satan is primarily, if not exclusively, in the culture or the world. This war with the culture has less of a focus on love and more of one on winning the battle. We are at war with the culture, but we can take pride that we are on the winning side. This pride is what fuels the arrogance of some within the body of Christ. When we set out to witness to others, we come with anger and pride instead of humility and love. I've been to Christian concerts and conventions on many occasions where artists and speakers seem to be yelling and scolding those in the audience who are listening. I'm so grieved by the lack of love coming from the platform.

Some Christians have an approach to evangelism that basically takes people to the whipping post. It seems in the Gospels that when Jesus became angry or took people to task, His primary focus was on the religious leaders who had corrupted God's message. Jesus had confrontations with self-serving and arrogant religious leaders who in some cases seemed to put themselves in the place of God. But when Jesus was among the lost and those whom the religious leaders looked down on, He expressed compassion and love. Could it be that as we look at those in the culture, we don't see them with the eyes of God?

Could it be that we see those in culture this way because we have a warped view of who we really are in Christ? I believe if we saw ourselves as the beloved, we would see the culture around us differently. Maybe looking at the culture and those in it primarily as the enemy is connected to a warped view of how God looks at us. Going a little deeper, how do you think God looked upon you before you became a Christian? Seriously? If God looked upon us with tremendous love before we were Christians, how should we now as believers look at God's creation and those within it? Notice, I just exchanged the word *culture* with *God's creation*. God is the Creator of the heavens and the earth. Yes, through sin God's creation has been corrupted. And yes, there is an Evil One who seeks to rule over what was created by God. But in the meantime we are called as God's beloved children to advance the beloved world, to be a part of His Kingdom coming and His will being done. Our war is primarily against an enemy in the spiritual realm, not the culture.

> *For our struggle is not against flesh and blood, but against the rulers, against the powers, against the world forces of this darkness, against the spiritual forces of wickedness in the heavenly places.*
>
> **Ephesians 6:12**

The problem with seeing culture primarily as the enemy is that the focus of our war against the culture gets focused too easily on the people within it. When this happens, we make those outside of the church and the Christian life the enemy. Jesus is very clear on what to do when people become our enemies; we are to love them (Matthew 5:43–45).

To see culture as the enemy is not the right approach, but neither is a full embracing of the culture. Some parts of the church have embraced the culture around them to the point that they have lost touch with enduring values, which are essential to advancing the beloved world. We must be careful about an embracing of the culture that causes us to question or totally move away from the authority and centrality of Scripture. The biblical approach to culture is not about painting it as the enemy or fully embracing it. The biblical approach is to engage culture for Kingdom purposes. This is what leads to advancing the beloved world. In the gospel of John, Jesus speaks to the Father about how His followers ought to live in the world, the culture around them.

> *But now I come to You; and these things I speak in the world so that they may have My joy made full in themselves. I have given them Your word; and the world has hated them, because they are not of the world, even as I am not of the world. I do not ask You to take them out of the world, but to keep them from the evil one. They are not of the world, even as I am not of the world. Sanctify them in the truth; Your word is truth. As You sent Me into the world, I also have sent them into the world.*

John 17:13–18

We are in the culture, and we may even face opposition, but Jesus asks the Father that He keep us from the Evil One. Jesus also says that we are not of this world. We are in the culture but not of it because our identity is in Christ and we are citizens of the Kingdom of God. As we read on in the chapter, He calls us as His followers into oneness.

> *I do not ask on behalf of these alone, but for those also who believe in Me through their word; that they may all be one; even as You, Father, are in Me and I in You, that they also may be in Us, so that the world may believe that You sent Me.*

John 17:20–21

Jesus was thinking not only of those following then but also of those who would come to know Him as Savior after He was no longer physically with them. Could He also have been mindful of those who would come to know Him generations later because of this? Through the testimony of their word passed down generation after generation, Jesus lifts up a desire to the Father that we would be one as He and the Father are one. In the cultural reality of ethnic and racial diversity, the body of Christ seeking oneness across ethnicity and race is essential. Experiencing unity and love as empowered by God is a critical part of the beloved church.

> *The glory which You have given Me I have given to them, that they may be one, just as We are one; I in*

them and You in Me, that they may be perfected in unity, so that the world may know that You sent Me, and loved them, even as You have loved Me.

John 17:22–23

The beloved church shouldn't be divided by race, ethnicity, or class because it affects our ability to engage the culture around us for Kingdom purposes. Scripture gives us many examples of engaging culture for Kingdom advancement. In John 17, we see that we are to be in the culture (world) and extend God's love within it as a unified body carrying God's glory.

◆ ◆

As we think about the culture we are in, it's good to begin by considering the cultural influences around us; multiethnicity, technology, youth, hip-hop, and urbanization are just a few. There are even subcultures within cultures. You have to consider where God has placed you, the gifts God has placed in you, and the call God has for you. For me, in an urban context, this has led me to a passion and call to engage the urban subculture known as hip-hop.

Hip-hop culture is seen by some as only rap music. But it is much more than that. It is a cultural movement and global influence. The culture of hip-hop contains language, fashion, values, and a broader art form, including dance and graffiti. Hip-hop is influencing youth and young adults not only in U.S. cities, suburbs, and rural areas but also in places such as South Africa, Japan, England, and Russia.

Hip-hop culture was born in the Bronx area of New York as an alternative artistic and social expression of urban youth. The original elements are the deejay, the rapper, the B-boy or B-girl (also known as the dance form breaking), graffiti art, a knowledge of self, and a knowledge of God. Yes, that's right, one of the original elements of hip-hop culture is having knowledge of God in order to truly know yourself! The original principles of hip-hop are peace, love, community, unity, and having fun. Some of the pioneers of this culture saw the creation of this nonviolent movement as the primary means to solve conflict, drug dealing, and the mistreatment of women. Ironically, today's commercial rap music actually glorifies the very things that the hip-hop culture was originally against.

As one who grew up in the church and in hip-hop, it has been sad for me to watch the way the church in general has responded to this culture. The response of many churches in the United States has been to paint hip-hop culture as the enemy, as an invention of Satan with the purpose of getting youth to worship evil instead of a holy God. This perspective is held because many can't see hip-hop beyond commercial rap, which is full of negative and stereotypical images of African American and urban culture: glorifying gang life, pimping, alcohol and drug abuse, and prostitution. The worst of this has been bonded with a corporate entertainment machine that places money over morality. If it weren't for the fact that these rappers clothed in stereotypes were making money, it would be more obvious that commercial rap is the new cotton and the mainstream rap industry is the largest plantation in the United States. The money and access to celebrity status cover up this slavery of art. It's no coincidence that the Dirty South style of rap is the most popular. Slavery in America is historically a Southern economic system, and Dirty South rap seems to have replaced cotton plantations very well. I've talked to people in marketing who have said, "In many ways the commercial rap industry markets through negative images and stereotypes of African American and urban youth in order to market to a mostly suburban youth audience." This is why Christians everywhere ought to care about the state and influence of hip-hop culture.

If hip-hop is nothing more than Dirty South rap and not a broader, global, influencing culture, then the church is correct in painting it as a demonic force that does more harm than good. But this is simply not the case. The major problem is really one of ignorance; the church doesn't know the real history, elements, and principles of the culture. I have great passion about this subject, and I believe the church must seek to understand hip-hop as a culture. If not, then all of the church's rhetoric about caring for people is just empty words. Hip-hop is a harvest field full of youth and adults who are hungry for identity, relationship, and community. When you think of all who are influenced by this culture, the millions of lives, it is simply amazing!

So where does one start? How about with the original elements and principles of hip-hop culture? It should be a no-brainer: peace, love,

community, unity, and having fun. Take the principle of peace, for
instance.

> *Blessed are the peacemakers, for they shall be called*
> *sons of God.*

Matthew 5:9

Peace is a great place to start because so much of today's commercial rap industry is about the promotion of violence. Through
images and storytelling centered on hustling, gang affiliation, drug
dealing, and prostitution, violence is glorified. We have the opportunity to engage hip-hop culture by being an extension and expression
of the peace of God.

One of the pioneers of holy hip-hop culture was a group
known as Preachers in Disguise. They later became known as simply
Preachas. One of the members of this group is a good friend of mine,
Fred Lynch. Fred recently came out with a hip-hop translation of
the book of John called *The Script*; he's also a hip-hop theologian.
One of the Preachas' first singles was entitled "Let Me See Your
Fruit." This song spoke to the fruit that comes from advancing the
Kingdom of God through evangelism, but also through lifestyle
choices. Hip-hop ministries, like Preachas, that connect the
principles of hip-hop with the fruits of the Spirit in Scripture create
Kingdom movements. If hip-hop culture is truly as influential as
I'm proposing it is, just think of the global Kingdom-advancing
potential that exists in engaging this culture. The church cannot

afford to write off hip-hop culture as the enemy. Instead we must be willing to jump into hip-hop.

Because of the impact of hip-hop in the city, this is especially true for the urban church. I was blessed to have pastored a church in Minneapolis that was and still is an evangelical, hip-hop, multiethnic, missional, relevant, and urban community. Sanctuary Covenant Church puts on a monthly hip-hop worship experience, runs the Hip-Hop Academy—an after-school program that teaches the real history, elements, and principles of hip-hop culture—and provides classes to help people understand various urban subcultures and how we are to engage them. I would not call Sanctuary just a hip-hop church. Sanctuary is a Christ-centered community that has a desire to see the Kingdom of God made manifest within urban subcultures such as hip-hop. It is not the only beloved church taking the jump into hip-hop culture; there are others, such as Shiloh Temple Church in Minneapolis, the House Covenant Church in Chicago, and Crossover Church in Tampa, Florida.

Maybe hip-hop isn't the major cultural influence around you. If so, that's okay. Ask yourself what is. And then engage whatever cultures are the major influences around you in order to advance God's Kingdom. Whatever the culture may be, we've got to be willing to jump.

Chapter 7

THE CITY

Then I saw a new heaven and a new earth; for the first heaven and the first earth passed away, and there is no longer any sea. And I saw the holy city, new Jerusalem, coming down out of heaven from God, made ready as a bride adorned for her husband.

Revelation 21:1–2

With every passing day, the world around us is becoming more multicultural and more urban. What used to be farmland is now a suburb. What was once a suburb now looks like a city. Cities are expanding into larger metropolitan areas connecting intimately, or so it seems, with first- and second-ring suburban areas. This has created a multiethnic, urbanized, technological, fast-paced world. Diversity is what we are; it is the reality. At the same time, the American church is in crisis. Many mainline Protestant denominations are dying, especially those in the city. As the city is getting bigger and more diverse, the church is getting smaller. I don't see this as a reason for the church to throw in the towel. I see it as an opportunity for the church to jump.

Why is engaging the city so important? Well, for one, the place where we will live eternally as God's beloved is depicted in Scripture as a city. In Revelation 21, John describes a new heaven and a new earth. He writes of a New Jerusalem, a holy city, where we will live eternally. In Revelation 7, we get a glimpse of what is going on in this eternal city and who is there.

> *After these things I looked, and behold, a great multitude which no one could count, from every nation and all tribes and peoples and tongues, standing before the throne and before the Lamb.*
>
> **Revelation 7:9**

In this city is a multicultural multitude, and the Lamb, Jesus, is on the throne. Jesus is the focal point of the city, the One who is able to create an intercultural oneness in this holy city. Jesus does there what government, the marketplace, and professional sports can never fully achieve in this earthly realm. Full unity and reconciliation flourish in that city. The people described in Revelation 7 experience not only oneness but also a deliverance from a "great tribulation." The things that plagued them in the earthly realm are no longer an issue in the eternal city. The chapter closes with this multicultural multitude worshipping day and night in the presence of the Lamb. It also states that they will hunger and thirst no longer. This isn't just about a hunger for food or a thirst for drink. They will no longer hunger or thirst for love, identity, belonging, or community. The beloved community in full can be experienced only in this great eternal city.

As we go once again to Revelation 21, John also speaks about the ultimate reality of this great city: We live forever. We escape the clutches of death through our citizenship in this heavenly city.

> *And I heard a loud voice from the throne, saying, "Behold, the tabernacle of God is among men, and He will dwell among them, and they shall be His people, and God Himself will be among them, and He will wipe away every tear from their eyes; and there will no longer be any death; there will no longer be any mourning, or crying, or pain; the first things have passed away."*
>
> **Revelation 21:3–4**

For the beloved of God, a great and eternal city awaits us one day. But what are we to do until then? Are we just to stay safe within the walls of the beloved church? Absolutely not! Remember, the life of the beloved is one of overflow. We are to be a force of the love, compassion, mercy, justice, and truth of God. This force cannot be fully contained by any human being. A pastor friend of mine once said something like this in a sermon: "When Jesus returns, He will bring ultimate justice, but until then, it's just us. Ordinary beloved children of God doing extraordinary works on behalf of the Kingdom."

◆ ◆

The truly beloved church cannot stay within a church building. The people must go out and advance the beloved world. This liberating life ought to begin in the cities closest to us. The cities around us are places of complex challenges, places with larger populations of the disenfranchised, the marginalized, and the hurting. It's true that challenges exist in our suburbs and rural areas and we should advance there as well. We have to see this in tension with the escape mentality from our cities over the last fifty years. This began with whites moving out of cities in the '50s, '60s, and '70s. This was followed by people of many different ethnicities leaving cities in the '80s and '90s and even continuing today. People (including myself) have left the city for the suburbs for many reasons.

Some have left pursuing an American dream that has come to include safety. Many people dream of a place where they don't have to lock their doors and they can keep their windows open. Others dream of a place where everyone knows each other and looks out for one another. I'm not sure if this "safe land" exists. Come to think of it, the Bible does not promise safety, but it seems it is the pursuit of many Christians I know. I must admit that I've struggled with this myself. I write this wrestling with my own passion for the city while living in a first-ring suburb.

I will never forget the day when my wife and I were living in the inner city just south of downtown Minneapolis. Soon after our first daughter, Jaeda, was born, two young men in our backyard were engaged in a shoot-out with a group of young men across the street. My wife, Donecia, grabbed Jaeda and fell to the floor. I went to the floor too. Donecia looked at me with tears in her eyes and said, "Do we have to live here?" We soon bought a house in north Minneapolis. We were still in the city and in a challenging neighborhood though. I came home one evening to find a group of young men sitting and standing in front of my house smoking weed and drinking beer. After heading inside, I looked out my front window at them and prayed about what to do. At the time I worked for the Minnesota Fellowship of Christian Athletes, which published a magazine called *Sharing the Victory*. I grabbed a bunch of the magazines and went out the front door, approaching the group. I introduced myself and started handing them out. They left so fast you would have thought I was the police!

When I served as senior pastor of the Sanctuary Covenant Church, my wife and I lived in a first-ring suburb of north Minneapolis. I worked and ministered in north Minneapolis as a pastor, and my wife worked at Minneapolis North Community High School. We wrestled with living in a suburb because we have always had a heart for the city. Today, we live in a suburb outside of San Francisco but still connect with people in many urban areas in states such as California, Nevada, and Arizona through my role as superintendent of the Pacific Southwest Conference of the Evangelical Covenant Church.

I believe all of God's beloved should wrestle on some level with how God is calling them to advance the beloved world in the city. The city, with all its challenges, must be a priority for us to some extent. Why is this so important? Because when Jesus walked the earth, He didn't avoid the cities closest to Him. Jesus engaged cities and proclaimed the Kingdom of God within them. He also addressed the issues and challenges of cities. As followers of Jesus, we must consider this; I don't believe we have an option.

◆ ◆

Jesus was going through all the cities and villages, teaching in their synagogues and proclaiming the gospel of the kingdom, and healing every kind of disease and every kind of sickness. Seeing the people, He felt compassion for them, because they were distressed and dispirited like sheep without a shepherd.

Matthew 9:35–36

We can learn a number of things from Jesus and how He engaged the city for the Kingdom cause. The Scripture says that as Jesus went from city to city and town to town, He saw the multitudes that resided in those places. He was able to see them because He was present with them in some manner. Even if we don't live in the city, we need to be present there somehow, seeking to see the multitude of the city on some level.

I also want to be clear that we are not taking the position that we, or our church, are bringing Jesus to the city. I told the Sanctuary congregation this when we first began in 2003 and I recently reminded them: "We did not bring Jesus to north Minneapolis, but we are joining Jesus, who was already in north Minneapolis before we began."

Jesus walked the earth engaging the cities closest to Him, proclaiming the Kingdom. He was advancing a beloved world. Matthew 9 gives a great picture of Jesus making an impact on the people of the cities and towns. Jesus took a man who was paralyzed and made him whole. As we engage the city, we must address those who are paralyzed. But in the cities today, this is often more than a physical state. The issues and challenges of living in the city can cause a paralysis of the heart. The woman raising children on her own, trying to financially support them and make sure they're doing well in school, may feel paralyzed. The unemployed man looking for a new job may feel paralyzed. Drug addiction can be a prison of paralysis. These people are looking for wholeness and healing.

Jesus also dealt with the corrupt economic system in the cities he engaged. He called out to the tax collector. The tax collector would have been seen as a traitor to the Jewish people, helping to support the economic system of the oppressive Roman Empire. Jesus sat down and had a meal with him. In today's cities, the beloved church must engage those who find themselves participating in a negative cash-flow system that oppresses those around them.

Jesus also stood in the crowd of the city, close enough that a woman with an issue of blood could touch Him and be healed. Though the city is crowded, we must be willing to stand among the multitude, close enough to touch and be touched. Jesus even addressed the issues of at-risk youth in the city. He engaged the life of a girl thought to be dead. But Jesus said, "She was just asleep" and told her to wake up, and she did! How can we as the beloved church speak to the lives of at-risk youth so they might know God's desires for them and wake up to their true purpose?

Jesus was present and actively brought the wholeness and healing of the great eternal city. In that city, the things that plague us, our tribulations, are dealt with.

> *These are the ones who come out of the great tribulation, and they have washed their robes and made them white in the blood of the Lamb. For this reason, they are before the throne of God; and they serve Him day and night in His temple; and He who sits on the throne will spread His tabernacle over them. They will hunger no longer, nor thirst anymore; nor will the sun*

beat down on them, nor any heat; for the Lamb in the center of the throne will be their shepherd.

Revelation 7:14–17

The beloved church must be salt and light among those in tribulation in the cities closest to us. We do this work because of God's compassion through us. Jesus not only saw the people of the city, but He had compassion for them. He didn't look at the people of the city and say, "What's wrong with you? Why don't you pull yourselves up by your bootstraps?" It may be debatable what the government should do with the people in our cities facing tribulation, but not for the people of God's Kingdom. We are to advance the beloved world among those struggling in the city. The issues of the multitude are numerous, and the people willing to help are usually few.

Then He said to His disciples, "The harvest is plentiful, but the workers are few. Therefore beseech the Lord of the harvest to send out workers into His harvest." Jesus summoned His twelve disciples and gave them authority over unclean spirits, to cast them out, and to heal every kind of disease and every kind of sickness.

Matthew 9:37—10:1

The challenge is often that those who make up the church may feel unqualified to engage the city for the Kingdom's cause. I firmly believe God will not call us to something that He will not empower us to do. Remember, Jesus empowered His followers to go out and do what He was doing before them. God has equipped us with talents, skills, and abilities in order to serve as Kingdom laborers. God has anointed you for His Kingdom cause. You are more blessed than you realize. You have what Evangelical Covenant Church theologian John Weborg calls "Kingdom Capital."

Oftentimes we don't feel as blessed as we really are because we define blessing American-style. So blessing from God is based on how big your house is, how expensive your car is, and how much money you make in your job. In other cases, being blessed is based on how happy you are. Thus the feeling of happiness, which can be so relative and driven by our flesh, becomes the barometer of blessing. Happiness, success, and safety may be American definitions of blessing, but we would be hard-pressed to see these as Kingdom definitions in Scripture. In the great eternal city where we will live, blessing and capital are redefined.

Here on the earth, we are blessed by God based on things (some more organic than physical) connected to the value system of God's Kingdom. Our prayers are a resource. Our praise and worship are also resources. Studying and applying God's Word in our lives is a resource. Our spiritual gifts are resources. Yes, our finances are a potential Kingdom resource too when connected to a holistic Kingdom economy of time, talent, and treasure. Our spiritual formation and growth are resources. All of this is Kingdom Capital that can be used in our Kingdom laborer portfolio. When you consider all of these resources belonging to the beloved of God, we soon realize that we are greatly blessed! In fact, we are blessed beyond measure.

God purposely blesses us more than enough so that we might be a blessing to someone else. He continually blesses us with Kingdom Capital that we might continually be a blessing to others. The problem with some of the theology in the prosperity gospel teachings is that so much of what is pointed to as being a blessing is based on the physical. So if you're not physically wealthy, based on the wealth structure of the United States of America, then you're not truly blessed. Not enough attention and value is placed on the invisible capital of the Kingdom, which carries more net worth for the beloved. The most valuable commodity we carry as the beloved is the Holy Spirit. This invisible resource is a great one to be used in advancing the beloved world in the city. Jesus Christ is the most valuable possession of the Kingdom, and because He lives in us through the Holy Spirit and we abide in Him, we are God's prized possession. Our value is found in Him. In Him we are righteous, we are holy, and we are victorious. We are blessed by God more than we can contain so that we might become blessings to others.

◆ ◆

I have a love for the city and people of the city. But even though I was born and raised in Minneapolis, I didn't always have a love for the city. You can live in the city and not have a love for that city and the people in it. When I became a Christian, God began to develop a love in me for the city and for the youth of the city. While in college, I worked every summer with middle school youth. After

I graduated from college, I began working as a youth minister at Rising Star Baptist Church. As a youth minister and basketball coach, I served in urban youth ministry for over twelve years. But you don't have to work professionally in urban ministry to make a Kingdom difference. You can volunteer as a tutor in the public schools. You can go to football or basketball games and cheer for kids by name. You can take prayer walks, and with each house that you pass, you can lift that family up in prayer. As an urban youth minister, I saw so many people use the gifts God gave them to make an impact on the city. Even today as a senior pastor, I continue to have a heart and passion for the transformation of lives in the city.

I'm happy for my time at Sanctuary Covenant Church when I was a pastor in an urban environment. I got to see so many people living out their love for the city. I think of Jeremiah and Vanessa Gamble, members of Sanctuary, who live in north Minneapolis with their three children. Jeremiah and Vanessa have a ministry called Theater for the Thirsty. They use their gifts of music and theater to give people a picture of God's Kingdom at camps and conferences. Vanessa leads worship at Sanctuary a few Sundays a year. The Gambles have said yes to connecting the great eternal city to the city closest to them.

A few years ago Jeremiah thought of a unique way to spend his birthday. Instead of a party being thrown for him, he decided to throw a party for his community. He asked friends and family members to help him with it. They set up grills on the corner of the block, giving out hundreds of hot dogs and hamburgers. They had a deejay playing holy hip-hop music. It seemed all Jeremiah wanted on his birthday was to see God's love have an impact on his neighborhood. Many families spoke of how this was the best event ever to take place in their community. All it took was Jeremiah understanding that he was blessed so much he couldn't keep it to himself.

We started the Sanctuary Community Development Corporation early on after we planted the church. Through this organization, which is an extension of the church, we have youth-development and workforce-development initiatives. The organization provides opportunities for members of Sanctuary's congregation, as well as partner churches, to participate in school-supply drives, tutoring, and mentoring. Soon after our church first started, we were serving a school that had kids being bused there from a homeless shelter. We didn't have the capacity to do something about changing their living situation, but we wanted to make sure they went to school with dignity. We made sure every kid had a new jacket, boots, gloves, and a backpack with school supplies. We have also provided teachers at urban schools with gift cards to show our appreciation for their work. We can't guarantee everyone we connect with will come to know Jesus as Lord and Savior. We don't do the saving anyway. What we can guarantee is that everyone has an opportunity to experience the love of Christ.

One day we will live in the great eternal city known as the Kingdom of God. In this beloved world, a multicultural multitude will worship the Lamb on the throne. Until then we are called to advance the Kingdom of God in the city closest to us. You have the opportunity to jump into the overflow of God's blessings on your life. Are you ready?

Chapter 8

MARRIAGE

Husbands, love your wives, just as Christ also loved the church and gave Himself up for her.

Ephesians 5:25

You might think a concluding chapter on marriage is strange for this book, but I believe it fits well. In fact, it is a snapshot of everything I've been talking about so far. When I think of jumping, I can't help but remember the day I married my wife, Donecia. We included in our marriage ceremony the African American wedding tradition of what is called "jumping the broom." Right after we were pronounced husband and wife, a broom was placed in front of us, and we jumped over it. And then we headed out of the sanctuary of Park Avenue United Methodist Church, where I first made the jump into God's love by accepting Jesus as my Lord and Savior.

Jumping the broom is a tradition used by some African Americans that dates back to slavery. During slavery in the United States, it was illegal for African slaves to marry. Not only was marriage illegal, but so was even learning to read. Many European Americans thought of African slaves in America as less than human. The specific view was that African slaves were only three-fifths human and might not even have a soul. And if they didn't have souls then they could not become Christians. If they were less than human, had no souls, and couldn't become Christians, then why not enslave them? African slaves had any sense of being loved by God taken away from them by an anthropology, sociology, and theology that together is arguably the original sin of the church in the United States of America. You could make a strong case about the treatment of Native Americans by the church as well. Be that as it may, slavery stripped the sense of the beloved self from Africans in America.

What is ironic, though, is the same religion that justified the enslavement of Africans in America also became the on-ramp for their liberation. It's like God wouldn't allow a Christianity to fully thrive that wasn't authentic to His Word. God would not allow a gospel to flourish that did not open up the possibility for all human beings to jump into the life of the beloved. It's interesting to me that when many evangelicals talk about the Kingdom of God spreading in other countries around the world, specifically in places where Christianity is illegal, they speak of underground churches. Early on in the development of this nation, African slaves empowered by God began to develop underground churches. In many cases at night, in the backwoods of the Deep South, African slaves empowered by the Spirit of almighty God were having church-worship experiences. African slaves experienced an underground revival of sorts that restored the beloved self through knowing Jesus as a Savior and a liberator. This is a miracle to me.

So, even though enslaved, African Americans supernaturally had access to the opportunity to jump into the beloved life. This occurred through underground worship experiences, which equipped and empowered African slaves to seek freedom in Christ. These worship experiences were the places where family was rebuilt as well. The opportunity to build a family was also illegal for African slaves. Even today when we look at some of the challenges facing the African American family, we cannot lose sight of the impact of slavery and, after that, Jim Crow segregation. To some degree, the fact that there are functional and stable African American families at all in the United States is a miracle. This miracle was established through marriage ceremonies within the underground church of African slaves. Though these marriages were in many cases not recognized by law, the belief was that they were by God. At the end of many of these wedding ceremonies a broom was placed in front of the bride and groom, and they would jump over it. This represented that, even enslaved, they could jump into a new life. The newly married couple jumped into a new identity as husband and wife. Could it be that this jump supernaturally dealt not only with going from being single to married but also with the false identity imposed by the system of slavery? Could it be that marriage, as ordained by God, could be a ministry vehicle to experience the beloved life?

◆ ◆

As I think about the journey of jumping with God, it's hard for me not to reflect continually on Donecia and me jumping the broom over seventeen years ago. It was much more than just symbolism of an African American tradition. I was mindful that there was a day when folks who look like me couldn't marry in front of a multiethnic congregation like we did that day. I thought about being able to trace my family tree on my mother's side back to a slave woman named Easter. That was a jump of liberation and new identity that Donecia and I made that day based on the miraculous work of a loving God through a people brought out of slavery. It's hard to take a marriage for granted when connected to this history.

Regardless of your ethnic and cultural background, though, none of us should take marriage for granted. Marriage is yet another opportunity to experience the advancing of the beloved world. Marriage ought to be seen as a ministry by all Christians no matter your ethnicity. The covenant of marriage is the first relational resource between human beings that God gave us to steward. In the first chapter of Genesis, we see God creating the heavens and the earth. He brings light into darkness. He creates day and night. He creates the sky, the land, and the waters. He creates so vegetation might come forth. He creates birds in the air, beasts on the land, and schools of fish and other sea creatures in the water. Then He creates man and woman in His image:

*God created man in His own image, in the image
of God He created him; male and female He created
them. God blessed them; and God said to them, "Be
fruitful and multiply, and fill the earth, and subdue
it; and rule over the fish of the sea and over the birds
of the sky and over every living thing that moves on
the earth."*

Genesis 1:27–28

God creates man and woman and gives them the mission of
stewardship, to manage that which doesn't belong to them. They are
told to be fruitful and multiply. Marriage must be seen as a beloved
ministry. Marriage is created by God as an outpouring of God's love
for Adam and Eve.

*Then the LORD God said, "It is not good for the man to
be alone; I will make him a helper suitable for him."*

Genesis 2:18

*The LORD God fashioned into a woman the rib which
He had taken from the man, and brought her to the
man. The man said, "This is now bone of my bones,
and flesh of my flesh; she shall be called Woman,*

*because she was taken out of Man." For this reason
a man shall leave his father and his mother, and be
joined to his wife; and they shall become one flesh. And
the man and his wife were both naked and were not
ashamed.*

Genesis 2:22–25

Marriage is an extension of God's love for us. It is a covenant that ought to be directly connected to and overflow from our covenant with God. Marriage is first and foremost about God and should be seen as a ministry. God created the covenant of marriage as a ministry between one man and one woman with the mission of being fruitful. This fruitfulness is about advancing God's love in the world.

Again, I call marriage a ministry because it is the first relational resource given to human beings to steward. Before pastors, prophets, priests, or apostles, there was the husband and the wife. Marriage is the first ministry that God developed to bear His name and express His love. Marriage is a beloved ministry through which we should be able to gain a glimpse of the beloved relationship that God wants with us. This is why having children within a marriage between a man and a woman is the best option because a child's first picture of God's love ought to be the love between the child's father and mother. Think of all the children who struggle with seeing themselves as God's beloved because they did not witness the beloved ministry of their father loving their mother. Though child rearing is not the only way that a married couple can advance God's Kingdom, it is a major way. A married couple adopting children as their own is a Kingdom-advancing act as well.

The problem with marriage today is that we've come to believe that marriage is primarily about us and not about God. Marriage unfortunately has been under attack ever since its creation as a ministry. Satan seems to be adamant in making marriage about us and not first and foremost about God.

◆ ◆

Now the serpent was more crafty than any beast of the field which the LORD God had made. And he said to the woman, "Indeed, has God said, 'You shall not eat from any tree of the garden'?" The woman said to the serpent, "From the fruit of the trees of the garden we may eat; but from the fruit of the tree which is in the middle of the garden, God has said, 'You shall not eat from it or touch it, or you will die.'" The serpent said to the woman, "You surely will not die! For God knows that in the day you eat from it your eyes will be opened, and you will be like God, knowing good and evil." When the woman saw that the tree was good for food, and that it was a delight to the eyes, and that the tree was desirable to make one wise, she took from its

fruit and ate; and she gave also to her husband with
her, and he ate.

Genesis 3:1–6

Satan wants us to question what marriage is by confusing the issue of stewardship within marriage. God created marriage and gave instructions to Adam and Eve. Their job was to be obedient to the mission and to the more detailed instructions surrounding that mission so they might be fruitful and advance the beloved world.

Satan's attack on marriage is centered on "It's about you, not God." When we adopt this philosophy, sin takes root. Many people get married believing that marriage is first and foremost about them, and they put their potential spouse in place of God. The belief becomes "Marriage will bring a love that will heal me, complete me, take me away from the pain of my childhood, rescue me from my parents' racism, help me fulfill my ministry call," and so forth. I've spoken on numerous Christian college campuses and heard stories of many students feeling depressed because by their senior year they hadn't yet found their future husband or wife. Going to Christian colleges to find a mate has trumped going there to grow deeper in God and in understanding His Kingdom purposes. Could this be why over half of Christian marriages end in divorce? Satan has led many Christians to a distorted understanding of marriage; it's seen as a relationship all about us.

Many books have been written, geared toward Christians, that feed into this. These books may mention God and even provide some Scripture, but they focus on happiness in marriage or building a marriage free from adultery. It's not that these issues shouldn't be dealt with, but by just focusing on these alone, we lose sight of what marriage is all about. Marriage is a beloved ministry, developed as an extension of who God is, with the purpose of God being known through it.

◆ ◆

As I think about the marriage God has blessed me with, I realize that I need God in order to love Donecia the way God desires her to be loved. Now, let me back up so that you don't miss that I said *the marriage God has blessed me with,* not *my marriage.* This is important so we grasp that marriage is a ministry and blessing from God that we are given the responsibility to steward. The fine line for Christians is in losing sight of marriage as being primarily about God's love and it being extended throughout the world.

As a pastor, I've met so many young women in church who seem to be depressed because they're not in a relationship that is heading toward marriage. I'm not talking about women in their forties or fifties who feel like time is running out. I'm talking about young women right out of college who are jumping from one relationship to the next hoping this time marriage will arrive and they will finally be loved. I know this does not encompass all young Christian women in the church, but this is the story of far too many. I also realize the role that sexism plays in this. Sexism in the church looks like a mother and father who feel that their daughter must be married and give them grandchildren in order for that daughter to be more complete, almost more godly.

Outside the church these ladies are being bombarded by images within movies, music videos, and sitcoms of women needing a relationship in order for love to really blossom in their lives. This is not to let men off the hook, because it's men who drive and, in too many cases, find fulfillment in this sexism. The bottom line is the cultures inside and outside of the church work together to lead women to believe they are not really loved until they're in a relationship with another person. This is why putting God first even before marriage is so important.

Because the Bible states in Genesis 2 that God didn't want Adam to be alone, leading to the creation of Eve, we take this to mean that Adam would have been lonely without Eve. This is not true. This text is speaking to Adam not being alone within the mission of stewardship given by God. This is about a blessing of experiencing God's love, but it should not lead us to feel unloved while we plot to get married. Before jumping into the ministry of marriage, we must experience the truth of being loved by God first. This is about living daily in the beloved self. This jump must be made first, before the jump into beloved marriage.

This is so important because a beloved marriage, a marriage that is a ministry through which the beloved world can be advanced, is not possible without the empowerment that comes from the beloved self. This is why I made the statement that I cannot love my wife the way God desires her to be loved in my own power. I must begin with the truth that God can love Donecia better than I can. The best I can do is to allow God to love my wife through me. How does that happen?

It happens by my jumping into marriage with, or adopting after I've gotten married, the truth that I am God's beloved. I'm loved so much by God that the overflow of that love loves my wife. Christ in me, through the indwelling of the Holy Spirit, loves my wife. And Christ in my wife loves me. This awesome and amazing love creates another overflow, which is God loving through our marriage in order to affect our children and the world around us. This is what makes marriage a ministry, but it's also why the Enemy attacks marriage so much. The Enemy's attack on marriage is not primarily about increasing the divorce rate as much as it's about keeping us from God's love. Satan's attack on marriage doesn't begin once we're married; it begins well before. Satan's plan from the beginning has been about making marriage self-centered instead of God centered and empowered. When marriage is centered on us, it loses its power to advance the beloved world.

◆ ◆

Far too many Christians avoid the jump into the life of the beloved self by hiding in their marriages. They are convinced that everything is okay because they've found "the love of their life." The problem is they haven't truly found the love "that brings life" and brings it to the full. This is why the divorce rate is what it is among Christians; we're trying to live out marriage in our own power, trying to get all of our love needs met with a relationship we've made all about us.

I'm so thankful that Jesus Christ, the greatest expression of God's love for us, restores marriage to its rightful place. In coming to establish the church, Jesus also restores the beloved marriage. Isn't it interesting that within Scripture the relationship between Jesus and the church is compared to a marriage? It's also interesting that the relationship between God and the nation of Israel as well as between God and the world is compared to a marriage. Marriage as a metaphor within Scripture is about the advancement of the beloved world and points to the beloved marriage simultaneously.

Consider Scriptures within the New Testament that deal with the church and love; these can be connected to marriage and love because marriage is a ministry. Let's look at Philippians 2, for instance:

> *Therefore if there is any encouragement in Christ, if there is any consolation of love, if there is any fellowship of the Spirit, if any affection and compassion, make my joy complete by being of the same mind, maintaining the same love, united in spirit, intent on one purpose. Do nothing from selfishness or empty conceit, but with humility of mind regard one another as more important than yourselves; do not merely look out for your own personal interests, but also for the interests of*

others. Have this attitude in yourselves which was also in Christ Jesus.

Philippians 2:1–5

What if we applied the biblical principles laid out here by Paul for the beloved church to the beloved ministry of marriage? Before we make the jump into marriage, we must reflect deeply on where we are with God. Paul starts out by asking us to look at where we are in our beloved relationship with God through Jesus and the indwelling of the Holy Spirit. Is there encouragement in Christ? Is there fellowship with the Holy Spirit? He's saying to the church at Philippi that if you are experiencing something powerful in your relationship with God, let it have an impact on your relationship with one another. Since marriage is a ministry, one created by God before He created the church, why not apply these principles? Whether you are married or desiring to be, let Philippians 2 lead you to rethink what marriage should be like. If you are experiencing love, affection, and compassion with God as an individual, then let God extend this into your marriage. If you are not experiencing this with God, you could be in or going into marriage as the broken, not the beloved. Some people want a loving marriage without having an even greater desire for a loving relationship with God first. Marriage ought to be a beloved man and a beloved woman extending God's love to one another. Their marriage then becomes a beloved marriage of "being of the same mind, maintaining the same love, united in spirit, intent on one purpose" (Philippians 2:2).

"Do nothing from selfishness or empty conceit, but with humility of mind regard one another as more important than yourselves" (verse 3). The beloved marriage begins with an intimate relationship with God. I call this first principle "I am the beloved." The second principle, then, is putting your spouse first. Let's call this "I put you first." The third principle comes from verse 7: "But emptied Himself, taking the form of a bond-servant, and being made in the likeness of men." From this verse comes the principle "I serve you." Looking at the very next verse we find another principle: "Being found in appearance as a man, He humbled Himself by becoming obedient to the point of death, even death on a cross" (verse 8). This principle is "I humble myself." Finally, in verse 18, Paul says, "You too, I urge you, rejoice in the same way and share your joy with me." This principle is "I rejoice." So, all together the biblical principles for the beloved marriage look like this:

- I am the beloved.
- I put you first.
- I serve you.
- I humble myself.
- I rejoice.

A beloved marriage, as two people rejoice together in God's love, has the opportunity to have an impact on others. This rejoicing doesn't mean that there won't be bumps in the road of the beloved marriage. Donecia and I had no idea where our jumping over the broom would take us. But we believed that God wanted to love us through each other, just like He wanted to love our children and our church and our world. Jumping into God's love has taken us far beyond anything we'd ever imagined. It is something that is eternal, everlasting, beloved. And it all started with a jump.

Bonus excerpt from …

YOU ARE GOD'S
Plan A

{and there is no plan b}

Dwight Robertson

David ⓒ Cook®

transforming lives together

YOU ARE GOD'S PLAN A
Published by David C. Cook
4050 Lee Vance View
Colorado Springs, CO 80918 U.S.A.

David C. Cook Distribution Canada
55 Woodslee Avenue, Paris, Ontario, Canada N3L 3E5

David C. Cook U.K., Kingsway Communications
Eastbourne, East Sussex BN23 6NT, England

The Web site addresses recommended throughout this book are offered as a
resource to you. These Web sites are not intended in any way to be or imply an
endorsement on the part of David C. Cook, nor do we vouch for their content.

Unless otherwise noted, all Scripture quotations are taken from the *Holy Bible,
New International Version®*. *NIV®*. Copyright © 1973, 1978, 1984 by International
Bible Society. Used by permission of Zondervan. All rights reserved. Scripture
quotations marked RSV are taken from the Revised Standard Version Bible, copyright
1952 [2nd edition, 1971], Division of Christian Education of the National Council
of the Churches of Christ in the United States of America. Used by permission. All
rights reserved; and KJV are taken from the King James Version of the Bible. (Public
Domain.) The author has added italics to Scripture quotations for emphasis.

The stories presented in this book are personal and include details
about the lives of family members, friends, and neighbors. While some
names and story details have been changed for privacy's sake, I've
sought to remain true to the essence and impact of each story.

LCCN 2009940961
ISBN 978-1-4347-6463-8
eISBN 978-1-4347-0189-3

© 2010 Dwight Robertson
Published in association with the literary agency of Wolgemuth & Associates, Inc.
First edition published by Kingdom Building Ministries in 2006
© Dwight Robertson and Mark Vermilion, ISBN 0-9788142-0-7

The Team: John Blase, Susan Tjaden, Amy Kiechlin,
Sarah Schultz, Jack Campbell, and Karen Athen
Cover Concept: Brand Innovation Group
Cover Design: Amy Kiechlin
Cover Photo: iStockphoto

Printed in the United States of America

Second Edition 2010

Introduction

Over many years, evangelist Billy Graham has earned respect from people of all faiths. But during the cold war era, at the height of the Brezhnev regime, he faced quite a bit of ridicule from conservatives in America for visiting the Soviet Union and meeting with leaders from the government and state church. "Why would Dr. Graham treat the enemies of America and detractors of the Western church with such courtesy and respect? Shouldn't he condemn Soviet human-rights abuses and their restraints on religious liberty?" they scoffed. One critic blamed him for setting the church back fifty years.

Upon hearing the accusation, Graham lowered his head and answered, "I am deeply ashamed. I have been trying very hard to set the church back *two thousand* years."

God's Plan A for redeeming the world was enacted two thousand years ago. But don't take that to mean the plan is irrelevant or outdated. God's plan is as relevant, powerful, and doable today as it was when Jesus enacted it.

But somehow over time, people have diluted, distorted, and even forgotten His plan. In order to understand it, then, we must press the rewind button and go back two thousand years to the days when Jesus walked the earth.

Really Seeing People

When I read the gospel accounts of Jesus' life and envision how He lived and ministered to the people around Him, I'm struck by the contrast to how most of us live our lives and approach ministry today.

When Jesus saw people, He didn't hurry past them—without noticing them—in order to get to His next meeting at the synagogue. He noticed people and their needs. He acknowledged them by slowing down and connecting with them in life-giving ways. He *saw* them and *stopped,* becoming God's extended plan of love and grace to those in need.

> Jesus went about all the cities and villages, teaching in their synagogues and preaching the gospel of the kingdom, and healing every disease and every infirmity. When he saw the crowds, he had compassion for them, because they were harassed and helpless, like sheep without a shepherd. (Matthew 9:35–36 RSV)

When people in Jesus' day used the word *saw,* they understood it meant not only seeing with the eyes but also perceiving and seeing below the surface to a person's thoughts and heart—to the person's true self. In fact, in Jesus' day, the distinction between seeing people on the surface and seeing people below the surface didn't exist. So this Scripture passage and others like it tell us that when Jesus saw the people around Him, He truly *saw* them, through and through.

Most of us don't. Not really.

"I See You!"

Not long ago, my son, Dreyson, started the school year at a new elementary school. When he returned home after the first day, I asked him how his day had gone.

"Awful, Dad," he moaned. "All the other kids already have their friends. They didn't even notice me. No one saw me at recess. No one sat by me in the school cafeteria. And no one talked to me in class or after school. I was *invisible,* Dad!"

An interesting word choice, isn't it? And yet, unfortunately, *many* people feel this same way. Every day they live overlooked, unnoticed, and unseen lives. "Invisible" seems to best express how they feel.

How often do we see people with our eyes but fail to see them past the surface? We may see them according to a category we've created for them or the role they play in our lives, but we often fail to discover anything else about them. *Seeing* a person as more than your neighbor—or the kid next door whose parents work all the time, or the guy in the cubicle next to you, or the checkout girl who bags your groceries—isn't easy. But none of those people should be categorized. They're real people with real lives and real stories. Unfortunately, most of us spend little time interacting with them. We barely even get to know their names, let alone any of the details of their lives.

It's time we slowed down and started seeing people like Jesus did. Or like people from the Zulu tribe in southern Africa do. Zulus greet each other by saying "I *see* you!" The response is "I am here!" What a powerful greeting!

Greet your servers by name (they usually wear a name tag) and ask them about their day. Encourage them. Tell them what you appreciate about their service. When you do, you'll be among the very few who *see* them.

And you'll be setting the church back two thousand years.

Beyond Seeing

Seeing is important. But Jesus didn't just see people. He *stopped* and served them. Seeing and stopping were two of the recurring hallmarks of His love.

He looked into the faces of children who weren't highly valued in society … and He stopped; He made the time to hold them on His lap.

When a man covered with leprosy fell to his knees and begged Jesus, "Lord, if you are willing, you can make me clean," Jesus *stopped* and touched him (Luke 5:12–13).

When He encountered a woman caught in adultery, He *stopped* and called her to a better life (John 8:1–11).

When faced with people oppressed and tormented by evil spirits, He *stopped* and delivered them (Matthew 8:28–34, for example).

When He encountered Matthew in his workplace, He *stopped* and began a long-term relationship with him (Matthew 9:9).

When everyone else ignored and walked past hurting people, Jesus didn't. He saw them and stopped.

Jesus never knew a stranger. Everyone belonged in one category: people to love. He valued others by asking them questions, discerning their needs, touching them, and serving them in practical ways.

Every changed life resulted from an engaging conversation with a stranger.

In the same way, we can follow in Jesus' footsteps by engaging strangers with a smile, an open heart, a word of encouragement, or even a spiritual deposit that could potentially change a life.

One Word

At one point, Jesus turned to His disciples and shared *with them one word* that explained why He stopped and saw in response to the needs around Him:

> Then [Jesus] said to his disciples, "The harvest is plentiful, but the *laborers* are few; pray therefore the Lord of the harvest to send out *laborers* into his harvest." (Matthew 9:37–38 RSV)

The word? *Laborers.*

It may not be a very glamorous word, yet it's what will set us back two thousand years to the way Jesus lived and ministered—and move us forward into a bright future, building God's Kingdom according to His Plan A. What the world needs, Jesus said, are laborers. Common, everyday laborers.

Laborers are Jesus' means for reaching the world with His love and forgiveness. They aren't just critical to His plan. They *are* His plan.

His only plan.

Kingdom *laborers* are God's Plan A.

But what exactly is a laborer? After all, it's not a normal household word people use to describe most Christians. After studying the word in Scripture, I've developed a simple definition: *Laborers are ordinary people who deeply love God and actively love others. They seek to live a life of love ... every moment of every day.*

A laborer is a minister—not just the professional kind like pastors and missionaries, but the common, ordinary kind like my wife (an art teacher) and children (students).

Laborers are everyday, everyplace ministers like my friend Shane, who works as a radio executive and leads some of his seeker friends and coworkers in a Tuesday-morning "breakfast club," sharing relevant Bible truth from his own life and helping them better discover God's amazing love and purpose for their lives.

Or like my friend Bill, who owns a large freight company and deeply cares for the welfare of his employees.

Or like my friends Norm and Becky, who served a short stint as overseas missionaries before unexpectedly returning home. They decided God must be sending them into a different kind of ministry. So, Norm pursued a career in sales, and Becky became a full-time mom. And, together, they became "missionaries" in their neighborhood, caring for and sharing with their neighbors in life-changing ways.

Or like James the Roofer, a special guy you will meet in the next chapter.

Laborers are ordinary people who express their love for God through practical, hands-and-feet service. They embody Jesus' primary means for reaching the world with His love. Because they live everyday lives in everyday society, they influence people in ways that few professional ministers could. And through their everyday jobs, they reach people who would never step foot in a church building.

Want to know what a laborer looks like? Look in the mirror. God has called *you* to be one.

And since laborers are God's Plan A for reaching the world, that means *you* are God's Plan A for reaching the world around you.

You are God's Plan A to the other soccer moms and dads you meet when you take your kids to practices and games.

You are God's Plan A to your coworkers, with whom you spend more hours than nearly anyone else.

You are God's Plan A in your neighborhood, where you have time and opportunities to develop natural and meaningful relationships with your neighbors.

You are God's Plan A in your high school classroom or college dorm.

You are God's Plan A at your favorite restaurant, where the servers know your name.

Not your pastor. *You.*

You are God's Plan A. (And did I mention there's no Plan B?)

Part One
THE PLAN

God has a plan
for loving and reaching the world—
it's *you!*

One
Overlooked and Undervalued

"Where did *that* come from?" I asked my wife, Dawn, as I rose from my recliner to take a closer look at the nasty water spot I had just noticed on the entryway ceiling of our home.

"We had some really intense thunderstorms yesterday," she explained, staring at the ugly spot. Apparently the combination of high winds and quarter-sized hail had taken its toll on our roof over the weekend while I was gone.

Dealing with a leaky roof was the last thing I wanted to tackle following a hectic weekend. After a full speaking schedule and then flight delays, missed connections, and turbulence on the way home, I just wanted to relax.

However, when Dawn said another round of storms was forecast to hit that week, I knew the work needed to be done that day. Feeling a bit nervous about hiring someone I knew nothing about—and yet knowing I didn't have much of a choice—I grabbed the Yellow Pages and the phone and started dialing. Seven calls later, I found someone who could fit me into his schedule. When this roofer, James, answered the phone, his reassuring voice and polite manner immediately put me at ease. He told me he could be at my house in four hours.

Right on time, the doorbell rang. Opening the door, I was surprised to see a rugged-looking guy with long hair pulled back in a ponytail. I confess he didn't quite fit the mental image I had conjured up during our phone conversation.

After introducing himself and asking some questions about our problem, he returned to his truck, grabbed his ladder, and climbed up onto the roof to assess the damage. A few minutes later, he crawled back down and quoted me a price for the work. It was surprisingly reasonable. He said the job would take only two or three hours, and he could do it right away. I agreed to the price, and before long, he was back on the roof, making the repair.

About an hour later, I heard a knock on my door. I cringed, thinking it was too soon for him to be done. As I opened the door, I thought to myself, *He's probably going to say that the damage is much worse than he expected—and that it's going to cost a lot more than he quoted.*

"All done!" James announced. "It shouldn't give you any more problems. If it does, just give me a call." Then he handed me a bill at a price that did not match his original quote. It was much *less*.

"I finished your roof quicker than I expected," he said. "So I only charged you for the actual time it took to complete the job."

Thankful for his honesty, I went to my home office to retrieve my checkbook. When I returned, James was talking to another customer on his cell phone. As I wrote out the check, I listened to his interaction with the other person. He treated her with the same professionalism and courtesy as he had treated me.

"Don't ever hire an answering service," I said as I handed him his check. "You really do a great job interacting with your customers on the phone. You have a way of quickly gaining people's confidence."

Then something unexpected happened.

He humbly looked at the ground for a moment, and then he looked me straight in the eyes and said, "Thank you for your kind words, but to be honest, I haven't always been good with people."

"What do you mean?"

"I made some pretty bad choices when I was younger. But about thirteen years ago, God caught my attention, and I began a personal relationship with Him. My life really changed after that. I'm a very different person than I was before."

As he shared some of the changes that had transpired in his life, he occasionally looked down and shook his head, still amazed at the work God had done.

"My desire is to serve God every day by serving my customers with kindness and respect," he explained. "I treat every roofing job as a daily assignment from God."

He spoke so openly about God that I glanced around to see if something had given him a clue that I was also a Christian—like a Bible lying within view. Nothing was there that would tip him off, so I said, "James … brother … hey, I'm a Christian too."

James' face lit up. He was excited to discover that we shared a common faith in God. And I was thrilled to find someone who lived out his faith so naturally in the everyday moments of his work life.

"Do you realize you're going places where few pastors could go and reaching people with your personal story that few pastors could reach?" I asked.

"You know, I've been thinking about that a lot," he replied, "but I've never heard anyone talk about it that way."

"James, God has uniquely positioned you to minister to others!" I continued with a growing sense of excitement. "You remind me of how Jesus ministered when He was here on earth. Most of His ministry took place *outside* the synagogue walls. He met needy people and served them where *they* lived. James, that's what you're doing!"

By that time, Dawn and our two children, Dara and Dreyson, had entered the room. I asked if we could pray for him and his ministry. He agreed, and so our family surrounded James the Roofer and placed our hands on his shoulders.

"Lord," I prayed, "we commission James for ministry. We pray for James just as church leaders would do for missionaries before sending them out to their fields of service."

His body trembled under our hands as we prayed. Then he began sobbing, which I didn't expect from such a rugged guy. Teardrops fell on the hardwood floor, literally forming a small puddle. As we concluded, James needed a moment to regain his composure.

"I'm sorry for crying," he said while sniffling. "It's just that no one has ever treated my ministry as if it's important. For the past thirteen years, I've believed that this is how God has chosen for me to represent Him to others—and in all that time, no one has ever validated that what I do for Him is important."

James went on to explain that he regularly prays that God will send him customers who need to hear about Jesus. Then he prays for each of them by name and asks God to give him opportunities to minister to them. He told us about one of those opportunities:

"A few years ago, I was working on the roof of a home in inner-city Denver. Suddenly a gunshot sounded from inside the house, and then I heard a scream. I scrambled off the roof and ran inside to find an older man lying on the floor in a pool of blood. His family had already called 911, but it was clear the man wasn't going to survive.

"Knowing that this may be his last chance to spend eternity in heaven with Jesus, I knelt down next to him. He couldn't move, but he locked his eyes on me.

"'Sir, God loves you very much. Do you want to know if you're going to be with Him in heaven when you die?' I wasn't sure if the man could hear me. He couldn't talk or move his body, but he could move his eyes up and down as if he were nodding his head. That moment, I led the man into a relationship with Christ by asking him questions and allowing him to continue answering with his eyes. He died a few moments later."

As James finished his story, I looked around at Dawn, Dara, and Dreyson. We were all fighting back tears. Before this holy moment ended, I asked James for his business card and told him I'd place it on our refrigerator next to the other prayer magnets for our missionary friends. Then our family promised James that we would pray for him and his ministry. Although we haven't seen him since that day, we still pray for him.

Then he thanked us repeatedly as he walked out our front door.

After my chance encounter with James the Roofer, I returned to my recliner to reflect on our exchange. God began deeply stirring and convicting my heart. I was grieved because James felt so overlooked and undervalued in his ministry to others. Week after week, he sat in church services that validated "up-front" and "specially called" people in their ministries. But no one had ever validated or commissioned James into the ministry that God had called him.

I thought about the countless people who must feel the same way—the nameless, faceless followers of Jesus who serve Him in ordinary ways in their ordinary lives. But, tragically, no one notices, validates, or affirms their faithfulness. No one notices that their ministries are extremely important to God.

Yet the Bible clearly shows us that God chooses and uses ordinary people like James the Roofer to do the extraordinary work of His Kingdom in the ordinary venues of life.

He always has. He still does. And we have every reason to believe He always will.

Where was it along the way that we lost track of Jesus' plan? When did we become so preoccupied with our own modern methods that we stopped recognizing and valuing the extraordinary work God performs through ordinary people? Instead, we've become enamored with "professional" ministers (people who make a living from their ministry service) and Christian celebrities (the highly gifted few who serve in ministry spotlights and on ministry platforms). We point to these people and methods as the standard for what it means to do something important for God.

But the day-to-day ministry of faithful servants like James the Roofer is at the heart of God's plan for reaching the world.

It's time to take a closer look at what God says in His Word about the nature of ministry and who's called and qualified to do it. Jesus chose the ordinary. He validated the weak. He called out the imperfect. He honored the poor in spirit. He sought after the humble of heart. And He gave them all a significant role to play in His Kingdom work.

If you've avoided involving yourself in the work of God's Kingdom because you don't think you have anything significant to contribute, then I have good news for you: God *wants* to work through you. He *chooses* you.

Perhaps you're like James the Roofer—you faithfully serve God in His Kingdom work, but you feel overlooked, undervalued, and maybe even unimportant. I have good news for you, too: God highly values your service to Him, regardless of the recognition you might receive. His announcement to you right now is "*You* are My plan!"